# Madrid

Footprint

*Mary-Ann Gallagher*

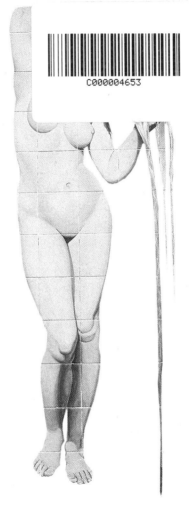

**Listings**

# About the author

Mary-Ann Gallagher graduated in modern languages from St Andrew's University and (having failed to catch her prince) went around the world instead. She has contributed to numerous guidebooks, mainly dealing with Spain, and writes regular travel articles for websites and magazines. She is author of the Footprint's Barcelona Handbook and is currently living in Spain researching for the Footprint Handbook to Spain. When not in Spain she lives in London but is happiest with a cocktail in Plaza de Chueca.

# Acknowledgements

Huge thanks to Yolanda, Guillermo, Susannah, Angel, Rosa, Matías and the boys from EL Cañi.

Madrid is not a city of half-measures: Europe's highest, greenest, youngest, sunniest capital likes to boast *Desde Madrid al Cielo* ('from Madrid to Heaven'), with its assumption that when you've seen Madrid, the only place left is Heaven. The city is as famous for what it lacks as for what it boasts – there's no great river, no architectural marvels, no immediate picture-postcard charm. But what it does have, it has in spades: a fabulous collection of western art held in the Prado, the Thyssen and the Reina Sofía, a crooked old centre where almost every alley is stuffed with excellent tapas bars and restaurants, and an intense nightlife that makes most other cities look staid and past it. Madrid can seem like several cities rolled into one: each *barrio* or neighbourhood has a distinct flavour, so you can swank around Salamanca one night, enjoy the populist buzz in Santa Ana the next, and finish up with an underground club in trendy Chueca or up-and-coming Lavapiés.

## Todo sobre mi Madrid

Madrid was just an uneventful country town back in 1561 when Felipe II proclaimed it Spain's new capital. Set high on a baking plain, the city appealed to Felipe because it was slap-bang in the centre of Spain (although the excellence of the hunting may also have had something to do with what everyone agreed was an idiosyncratic choice). Its Golden Age was the 17th century, when gold and silver poured in from Mexico and Peru, Cervantes published *Don Quixote* and Velázquez was appointed court painter to the Habsburg kings. Madrid looks best in close-up; take an aimless stroll and stumble across an outrageously lavish doorway, a Moorish flourish on a former belltower, or a boho-chic café in an old pharmacy. The Spanish gift for combining tradition and modernity with such effortless aplomb reaches new heights in Madrid, a city in which miracles can still happen (just visit the Church of Jesús de Medinaceli on the first Friday of the month) in one part of the city, while a glossy new nightclub is being toasted in another.

## Bohemian rhapsody

Nowadays the city has a split personality: on the one hand it's the political, artistic and royal centre of Spain with all the fancy trimmings (palace, parliament and opera house); on the other, it's an overgrown market town where everyone knows everyone else's business. And they'll want to know yours too; Madrileños are famous for their directness (or rudeness, according to out-of-towners). This is simply a desire not to waste time on small talk, but to concentrate on the real business of having a good time. This is where Madrileños excel and there can be few cities that radiate such vitality. There are thousands of tapas bars, flamenco clubs and cafés, but it's in the packed streets – especially after the Rastro flea market, or in the early hours of a hot summer's night – that the uniquely Madrileño gift for enjoying life really shines out.

# At a glance

### Paseo del Prado

The leafy, elegant Paseo del Arte sits on the eastern side of the city, where the three big museums – the Prado, the Centro de Arte de Reina Sofía, and the Thyssen-Bornemisza – are conveniently clustered just a short stroll apart. It's a hushed district of fine restaurants and private apartments and a smattering of smaller, dustier museums that provide back-up for the stellar charms of the Big Three. Behind the Prado stretches the luxuriant expanse of the Retiro Gardens, filled with ponds and fountains, glassy pavilions and rose gardens; a cool refuge from the summer heat.

### Santa Ana

West of the Paseo del Arte is the engaging *barrio* of Santa Ana, its narrow, sloping streets lined with traditional, tiled tapas bars and restaurants. It's been an earthy, cheerfully bohemian neighbourhood since the days of Cervantes and Lope de Vega when theatres and brothels vied for custom, and it still comes into its own after nightfall when the crowds flow around the Plaza Santa Ana and fight for space at the terrace cafés. By day it's quieter, and older locals sit on benches and watch in bemusement as the neighbourhood's new wave of arty, young professionals walk their designer pooches.

### Plaza Mayor

This square is the heart of old Madrid, an imposing ceremonial square where kings were crowned and heretics burned, now, sadly, given over to the kind of cafés which have plastic menus in a dozen languages. The crooked lanes which wind off the square are the city's oldest, the last dim echo of Madrid's Moorish past. They are lined with churches, convents and palaces, and traditional traders like classical guitar-makers and knife-sharpeners, all seemingly oblivious to the passing of time. To the east is the

Palacio Real, a dizzying whirl of baroque magnificence, and the city's beautifully restored Opera House.

## La Latina and Lavapiés

These traditional working-class neighbourhoods are spread chaotically downhill from the Plaza Mayor. Much of the area is shabby and dilapidated – although gentrification has definitely set in – but it's got an edgy vibrancy all of its own. Immigrants from North Africa and South America, authentic Madrileños and trendy young artists opening up bars and cafés make for an appealing mix. Don't miss the famous Sunday morning flea market, El Rastro, and follow it up with a tapas crawl.

## Gran Vía, Chueca and Malasaña

The Gran Vía swoops across the north of the old city, connecting east and west in a broad avenue lined with flamboyant 19th-century cinemas, banks and shops. The neighbourhoods to the north of the Gran Vía – Chueca and Malasaña – have got split personalities: sweetly old-fashioned by day, and unstoppably wild by night. These are the hippest areas, bursting with ultra-trendy shops and bars and famous for non-stop nightlife. Chueca is the heart of Madrid's gay scene and currently the most fashionable neighbourhood in the city.

## Salamanca

Swanky Salamanca in the northeast of the city is an elegant grid of broad avenues lined with chi chi apartments and upmarket restaurants. It oozes wealth, from the designer boutiques of Calle Serrano to the Porsches parked outside the exclusive clubs. Hidden away among all this opulence are some delightful 19th-century mansions and fans of modern architecture will enjoy the glossy towers which line the Paseo Castellano.

# Trip planner

Madrid may not have much in the way of big museums, but those it does have pack a big cultural punch; the great art museums of the Prado, the Reina Sofía, and the Thyssen are among the finest in Europe. There's a host of smaller but equally appealing attractions from the spellbinding frescoes of the Goya Pantheon to royal convents crammed with treasures and old bones. But beyond sights, what Madrid's *really* good at is partying. The city feels more alive at night; in summer terrace cafés spill into squares and streets are crammed until dawn. Don't sightsee in the blazing heat of the afternoon; have a long lunch and sleep it off.

Madrid has plenty to offer at any time of the year. Nonetheless, as Madrid freezes in winter and burns in summer; the best times to visit are spring (especially May for the Fiesta de San Isidro, see Festivals and events), and in September when the summer heat has mellowed. Avoid August; traditionally it's holiday month, and many hotels, shops and restaurants close and the heat is almost unbearable. Flight prices vary little during the year, and fall October-November and January-February.

## 24 hours

Have breakfast on the Plaza de Oriente, with views of the Palacio Real. Spend a few hours seeing the highlights at one of the big three museums – the Goyas at the Prado, Picasso's *Guernica* at the Reina Sofía or the Italian Primitives at the Thyssen (see p39). Trawl around the old-fashioned tapas bars in the Plaza Santa Ana for lunch (see p50), followed by a siesta under the trees in the Parque del Retiro (see p43). Take a look at some of the new galleries springing up in trendy Chueca or go shopping at its quirky fashion boutiques and take a break in a laid-back café like *La Ida* (see p166). Soak up the atmosphere at a traditional restaurant like *Viva Madrid* (see p166) followed by flamenco at *Casa Patas* (see p156). Alternatively, check out the Madrid club scene: celebrity-spot at

★

Best

## Ten of the best

1 See some of Europe's finest art collections in Madrid's three most important museums – the Prado, the Reina Sofía, or the Thyssen-Bornemisza and take a break with a picnic by the beautiful Palacio de Cristal in the Retiro Gardens, p44.

2 Browse through the bargains at the Rastro flea market, do the traditional round of tapas bars and then hang out in one of the fashionable new bars like *Delic*, p164.

3 Take a stroll through the Parque del Oeste, past the 2,000-year-old Templo de Debod and the lovely rose gardens, and head downhill to find the beautiful Panteón de Goya, small but perfectly formed, p82.

4 Enjoy a drink on the terrace at Las Vistillas as the sun sets over the Sierras, p76. Follow it up with a glass of *cava* at the relaxed *Champañería Librería*, p146.

5 Explore the tranquil and intimate little Casa-Museo Lope de Vega and while away the afternoon with a book in its delightful garden, p51.

6 On a boiling hot day, sway out in the cable car to the Casa de Campo, take a stroll among the trees and hire a boat on the lake where you can cool off under the spray of the fountain, p82.

7 Treat yourself to *churros con chocolate* in the *Chocolatería San Ginés* after a hard night's clubbing, p142.

8 Watch the tapestries being made as they have been for centuries at the Real Fábrica de Tapices, p45.

9 See the Museo Cerralbo, a beautiful 19th-century mansion stuffed with a very personal collection of art, p78.

10 Feast on a Sunday lunch of roasted suckling pig in the lovely mountain town of Segovia, p99.

*Suite*, one of the hot, new designer restaurant-bar-clubs (see p161), or hop onto a podium at *Ohm* (see p204). Finish up with some traditional *churros con chocolate* at the *Chocolatería San Ginés* (see p142).

## A long weekend

With two to four days at their disposal, art fans can spend longer at the Triángulo del Arte museums. If you're in a sightseeing mood visit the over-the-top Palacio Real or spend some money in Salamanca's chi chi boutiques if you're not. A stroll through the Parque del Oeste and the Panteón de Goya is a wonderful way to spend a sunny afternoon, or you could hire a bike and make for the wild expanse of the Casa de Campo. Watch the sun set over the mountains from Las Vistillas (see p76), where there is a clutch of great bars and restaurants (try the *Champagnerí María Pandora* (see p164) or *Entrecajas* (see p144) and don't miss the Rastro flea market followed by the required tapas crawl on Sunday.

## A week

Seven days will give you a chance to explore some of Madrid's more offbeat sights, like the Museo Cerralbo or Museo Lazaro Galdiano, mansions stuffed with eclectic art collections; or the Fábrica Real de Tapices, where tapestries are made as they were in the time of the Habsburgs; or the delightful Museo Sorolla, devoted to the painter known as 'the Spanish Impressionist'. Try out some of the fancy gourmet tapas bars in the Austrias neighbourhood (west of the Plaza Mayor), splash out on dinner at *Zalacaín* (see p152), or catch a drag show at *Gula Gula* (see p135). Take a couple of day trips to the ancient cities of Toledo, Segovia and Avila; the latter two are set in the beautiful sierras which are surprisingly close to Madrid if you want to do a bit of hiking, mountain biking or even skiing.

# Contemporary Madrid

Madrid's most famous export is probably Real Madrid, one of the world's richest and most successful football teams. Second in the fame stakes is Pedro Almodóvar, the unconventional film director who has become the toast of Hollywood since winning an Oscar in 2000 for *Todo Sobre Mi Madre* (*All About My Mother*) . If parts of Madrid seem strangely familiar to you, it's probably because you've seen them before in his films: from the sleaze of the Rastro flea market to the grand arcades of the Plaza Mayor, Madrid is as much a 'character' in his work as his favourite actresses, 'las chicas de Almodóvar', who regularly appear in his films.

The *Movida Madrileña* was just getting into its stride when Almodóvar had his first commercial success with *Pepi, Luci, Bom* in 1980: the year before, Tierno Galván, a gentle, soft-spoken professor of Marxist philosophy, had been elected mayor of Madrid and culminated his address to the people with the now-legendary phrase 'You know what to do: get stoned and watch out!' (*Así es que ya sabéis: a colocarse y al loro!*). Madrid knew exactly what to do, and for the next decade the city was the hottest, wildest and most creative in Europe – and Almodóvar was capturing its zeitgeist on film. Music, fashion, art and design flourished in the newly liberalized climate (film scripts had been censored until 1976 and the word 'thigh' was banned from theatres) and the new socialist government poured money into the arts in its eagerness to redress the balance of the Franco years.

The party was too intense to last and the cracks were already showing by the end of the 1980s: as Almodóvar was making international news with the success of *Mujeres al Borde de un Ataque de Nervios* (Women on the Edge of a Nervous Breakdown) in 1988, the government was having its own breakdown after a series of corruption scandals. By 1991 the socialists had been ousted from Madrid's city council and the right wing Partido Popular (PP) took over. In 1996, it also won the general elections

**Picture perfect**
*One of the many traditional images to decorate souvenir racks on the pavements of Madrid.*

and José María Aznar, a decidedly unglamorous former tax inspector and great pal of Tony Blair's, became prime minister with a mandate to sort out the country's finances. Madrid – and all of Spain – has been undergoing some serious belt-tightening ever since. It seems to have worked: unemployment is down, incomes and standard of living are up, and Aznar was re-elected in 2000 with an overall majority. But, to the fury of many Madrileños, most of the budget cuts have been directed at the arts, with contemporary and community-level art being the hardest hit.

On top of that, the reactionary PP are also cracking down on what they view as the excesses of Madrid's legendary nightlife: the *botellones* – massive weekend gatherings of teenagers with plastic bottles full of a vicious wine and coke concoction – have been abruptly wiped out by recent legislation; and the notorious 'after hours' clubs – nightclubs which opened their doors at dawn or later – are a dying breed. Almodóvar complained that the city is on its way to becoming 'as boring as Oslo'. But he is no longer a cult figure with his finger on the pulse; success and, most importantly, fame in Hollywood, has removed him from the ranks of the underground hero. And besides, Madrid's capacity for having a good time goes way back – long, long before the crazy years of the *Movida* – and it seems unlikely that its spirit will be squashed so easily. Ernest Hemingway observed that 'nobody goes to bed in Madrid until they have killed the night' and he would find little to make him change his mind on a Saturday night in Chueca. Few Madrileños will begin the party on Friday night and keep it going until Monday morning as they did at the height of the *Movida*, but even on half-throttle Madrid is still more vital than most European capitals.

Spain has changed at a dazzling pace since the isolation of the Franco years. The pay-off for the privileges of becoming a fully paid-up member of the international community has been the unavoidable dilution of its popular culture. Like everyone else, the Madrileneños lap up generic TV programmes like *Gran Hermano*

(Big Brother) and *Operación Triunfo* (which made the formerly unknown David Bisbal a massive pop star) and the city centre is slowly emptying as mod cons win out over character and people move into brand new suburban flats.

Despite this insidious banalisation some of Madrid's oldest traditions are being revived. The Madrileños are well known for their gift of the gab and like to boast that they have elevated the art of talking to an art form. The *tertulia*, an almost untranslatable term for debate or discussion, was perfected 100 years ago when writers and artists gathered daily at celebrated cafés like the *Fontana d'Oro*, the *Universal* and the *Pombo* to expound at length over coffee and brandies. The *tertulia* rapidly became part of the city's fabric, an essential thread in the cultural revival which some compared to the Golden Age of Cervantes and Velázquez. Most of the famous literary cafés have long gone, with the exception of the shabby *Café Comercial* which has hung on in Chueca (now with the internet and fruit machines) and the elegant *Café Gijón* on the Paseo de los Recoletos. Both still host regular *tertulias* and the tradition is also being revived in the new, old-style cafés which have risen up in emulation of the old classics.

To qualify as a *tertulia*, a discussion should have no purpose save that of the sheer joy of conversation. On summer evenings there isn't a free bench to be found in the whole of the city as the locals find a shady spot to enjoy a chat with friends. It might start out with an enquiry into someone's health, but before long a juicy *tertulia* is in full swing as Spain's performance in the World Cup, the latest antics of the mayor José María Alvarez del Manzano, (whose ability to waffle is legendary), or the scandal surrounding a plastic image of the Virgin which has begun shedding tears are fully debated. No one cares if the plastic Virgin is a swizz, or if the Mayor was right all along – the important thing is the conversation. It will take more than TV (*la caja tonta*, or stupid box) to quash a Madrileño.

The easiest way of getting to Madrid is by air; flights are remarkably cheap, particularly if you shop around on the internet. Book well in advance to get the best deals. Most airlines have abandoned the restriction that travel must include a Saturday night stay. The high season is from mid-May to mid-September, except August, when Madrileños sensibly abandon their baking city to tourists. Prices can fall dramatically between November and February. Trains from Paris or other parts of Europe are scenic but take ages – although you can travel overnight on the comfortable and surprisingly inexpensive Elipsis trains from Paris. If you want to travel cheaply, the coach is an option, but the 36-hour journey from the UK is only for masochists or those with student cards entitling them to worthwhile reductions. If you drive, park the car when you get to Madrid; driving around the city is horrendous.

# Getting there

## Air

**From UK and Ireland**  Several airlines offer services between the UK and Ireland. Prices range from around £300-500 for a flexible return ticket from the UK with a scheduled flight on **British Airways** or **Iberia**, to £50-100 for a non-flexible return ticket with a 'no-frills' carrier like **EasyJet**. For rock-bottom prices it's best to keep an eye out for offers advertised in the national press; the best deals often mean booking some time in advance. Leaving it until the last minute means you could end up paying the same prices as those charged on scheduled flights. *Iberia* has direct flights from Dublin and Belfast, but with most other airlines you'll have to change somewhere in UK. Useful websites include: www.expedia.co.uk  www.ebookers.com  www.cheapflights.co.uk

**From Europe**  Several carriers fly between major European cities and Madrid, including some of the 'no-frills' airlines like **EasyJet** (which has direct flights from Geneva to Barcelona, where you can pick up a regular shuttle service to Madrid), and **Virgin Express** which flies directly from Brussels. Otherwise, the major national airlines like *Air France*, *Lufthansa*, *KLM*, *Air Portugal*, and *Alitalia* all offer flights from major cities to Madrid. Spain's own national airline, **Iberia**, has services from all major European destinations. **Air Europa** has direct flights from Milan, Paris, Rome and Zurich.

**From North America**  **Iberia** has direct flights to Madrid from most major US cities. Prices vary considerably depending on the season and how far you book in advance. From the east coast, count on paying from US$500 for the cheapest ticket in low season, to around US$1,000 for high season. Prices are higher from the west coast, between US$800-1,200. Consider combining a cheap flight to London (there are usually plenty of good deals) with a budget flight to Madrid; see above.

**Airlines and travel agents**

www.americanairlines.com **T** 1 800 433 7300 (USA)

www.aircanada.ca **T** 1 888 247 2262 (Canada)

www.air-europa.com **T** 0870 240 1501 (UK),
+34 902 401 501 (Spain)

www.airfare.com **T** 1 800 886 4988 (USA)

www.airfrance.com **T** 0845 0845 111 (UK),
+33 (0) 820 820 820 (France)

www.alitalia.it **T** 0870 0000 123 (UK), +39 848 865 643 (Italy)

www.britishairways.com **T** 0845 773 33 77 (UK)

www.continentalairlines.com **T** 1 800 231 0856 (USA)

www.delta.com **T** 1 800 241 4141 (USA)

www.dialaflight.com **T** 0870 333 4488 (UK)

www.easyjet.com **T** 0870 6 000 000 (UK)

www.expedia.com **T** 1 800 397 3342 (USA)

www.flightcentre.ca **T** 1 888 967 5331 (Can)

www.flights.com **T** 1 800 452 1443 (USA)

www.flyaerlingus.com **T**(01) 886 8844 (Eire)

www.flybe.com **T** 0870 567 6676 (UK)

www.flybmi.co.uk **T** 0870 607 0555 (UK), (01) 407 3036 (Eire)

www.iberia.es **T** 0845 601 2854 (UK), +34 902 400 500 (Spain)

www.klm.com **T** 0870 5074 074 (UK), +31 (0) 204 747 747 (Ne)

www.lufthansa.com **T** 0845 7737 747 (UK),
+49 (0) 1803 803 803 (Germany)

www.priceline.com **T** 1 800 774 2354 (USA)

www.ryanair.com **T** 0871 246 0000 (UK)

www.statravel.com **T** 0870 1600 599 (UK)

www.tap-airportugal.pt **T** 0207 630 0746 (UK),
+351 808 205 700(Portugal)

www.virgin.com/atlantic **T** 01293 747747 (UK),
1 800 862 8621 (USA)

www.unitedairlines.com **T** 1 800 589 5582 (USA)

*Airport information* Madrid's international airport is in Barajas, 15 km northeast of the city. It's currently being expanded and the new terminal T4 is due to open in late 2003. For the moment, there are three terminals: T1 for international flights, T2 for national and regional flights (note that *Iberia* and *Air Europa* also use this terminal) and T3 for the shuttle to Barcelona. The terminals are interconnected so it is easy to walk between them. Most services are in T1, which has ATMs, money changing facilities, car hire services, a post office, tourist information desks, a free accommodation service (for mid-priced and expensive hotels), and left luggage lockers. For general airport information T 91 393 6000 and for flight information T 902 35 3570.

Shuttle buses depart every 15 minutes between 0445 and 0145 from T1 and T2 for the Plaza de Colón in the city centre. One-way tickets cost €2.40. Journey times vary from 20 to 50 minutes depending on the traffic. Note that the Metrobús ticket (see p26) is not valid on this bus.

The metro is the cheapest way to get into the city; a single ticket costs just €0.90. The journey to the centre takes roughly 40–50 minutes. Get a Metrobús ticket (10 rides for €5, see p26) if you'll be using public transport during your stay. Taxi ranks are outside all arrival halls. A taxi into the city costs €15-20.

If you arrive at Madrid airport after midnight few services will be open. The cafeteria in T1 closes at 2300, and the shops, post office and information desks usually close at around 2200 or earlier. If you have pre-booked a car, a car hire representative should meet your flight, but check in advance. If you haven't booked accommodation, your best bet is to head for an area with several hostels clustered on one street (like Calle Hortaleza in Chueca or the streets around the Plaza Santa Ana).

## Car
Getting to madrid from the UK by car is not only timeconsuming, two to three days of steady driving, but it is also expensive.

Motorways charge expensive tolls in France and Spain and ferry fares (see below) can be high in peak season. Petrol costs considerably more than in North America but roughly the same as in France, Spain and the UK. All vehicles must be roadworthy, registered and insured at least for third party. The Green Card, an internationally recognized proof of insurance, is not compulsory but it is strongly recommended. EU driving licences are accepted throughout the EU; travellers from other countries may need an International Driving Licence. For more information, contact the AA (T 08705 500600, www.theaa.co.uk) or the RAC (T 08705 722722, www.rac.co.uk). In general, standard European road rules apply. The legal alcohol limit is a mere 0.05%, and foreigners can get an on-the-spot fine of up to €300 if they exceed this. The speed limit in built-up areas is usually 50 km/hr, 100 km/hour on major roads and 120 km/hr on motorways, or *autovías*.

## Coach
Compared with the good deals often available through the no-frills airlines, the coach isn't always a cheap alternative, moreover you have a hellish two- to three-day journey. **Eurolines**, 52 Grosvenor Gardens, London SW1, T 020-7730 8235, www.eurolines.com departs several times a week in summer (once a week the rest of the year) from London to Spain; the journey to Madrid takes between 26-36 hours. Fares start at around £90 one-way, and £75-150 return. Peak-season fares are slightly higher. There are good discounts for students, under-26s, senior citizens and children under 12. The main bus and coach station in Madrid is the Estación Sur de Autobuses, Calle Méndez Alvaro, T 91 468 42 00, metro Méndez Alvaro. Bus 148 or the metro will link you with Plaza Colón in the city centre.

## Sea
There are two ferry services linking the UK with Spain: **Brittany Ferries**, T 08705 360360, www.brittany-ferries.com, operate a

Plymouth to Santander service. **P&O Ferries**, T 0870 242 4999, run a twice-weekly service from Portsmouth to Bilbao. Prices range dramatically according to the season, but expect to pay between £350-750 for a car and up to four people. Crossings take between 24 and 35 hours depending on the route and season and you have to book some form of accommodation.

There are many services linking the UK and France: **Hoverspeed Fast Ferries**, T 08705 240241, F 01304 240088, www.hoverspeed. co.uk  Crossings between Dover-Calais, Folkstone-Boulogne and Newhaven-Dieppe. **P&O Portsmouth**, T 0870 2424999, F 02392 864211, www.poportsmouth.com  Portsmouth to Le Havre and Cherbourg. **P&O Stena Line**, T 0870 600 0600, F01304 863464, www.posl.com  **SeaFrance**, T 08705 711711, www.seafrance.com Dover–Calais crossings. The fastest way of crossing the Channel by car is with **Eurotunnel**, T 08705 353535, www.eurotunnel.com Prices for a flexible return ticket start at £130 if you depart before 0700. Journey time is around 40 minutes.

## Train

Trains from London to Madrid take at least a day with a change in Paris. **Eurostar** (T 0870 6000 0796 in UK, T 1-800 EUROSTAR in the US or T 91 547 8442 in Spain, www.eurostar.com  takes three hours from London Waterloo to Paris Gare du Nord. One direct train departs daily from the Gare d'Austerlitz in Paris for Madrid, taking about 14 hours. Prices vary enormously, depending on when you travel and how far in advance you book. They start from about £120 and go up to about £500. Trains arrive at Atocha Station in the city centre, which is on the metro line. There is a taxi rank outside the arrivals hall. Book at least 14 days in advance for the best fares. For more information and details of the various European rail passes available (only useful if you plan to make several long journeys), contact **Rail Europe**, 179 Piccadilly, London W1V 0BA, T 08705 848 848, www.raileurope.co.uk  or **Rail Europe US**, T 1-800-438 7245, www.raileurope.com

# Getting around

Almost all Madrid's sights are clustered in the centre an enjoyable stroll from each other. However, if you're in a hurry, the buses and metro are cheap, efficient and user-friendly. Just a few places – the museums dotted around the Salamanca district and the Ventas bullring, for example – are a bit further afield but they are all accessible by public transport. The city information line, T 010 (English spoken), gives transport information. For online information, including bus and metro maps, www.ctm-madrid. es provides information on suburban bus and rail services if you are planning a day trip.

## Bus

The bus system is efficient and easy to use. The main hubs for buses are Puerta del Sol, the Plaza de Cibeles, Plaza Isabel II and Plaza Callao. Each stop has a clear map. Get on at the front and pay the driver or date stamp your bus pass in the small machine. Leave by the middle doors. Buses run from 0600 until midnight and there is a night bus service, which runs more frequently on Friday and Saturday nights from the Plaza de Cibeles. You can get free bus plans from tourist offices, metro and bus stations, or at www.ctm-madrid.es A single ticket for one trip by bus costs €0.95, but the Metrobús ticket (which can be shared) costs €5 for 10 journeys on the bus or metro. You can get single tickets at metro and bus stations and the Metrobús ticket is also sold at tobacconists or *estancos*.

There are a couple of DIY sightseeing tours on the public buses. Take the number 2 bus from Plaza España, along the Gran Vía – where you should get a glimpse of the famous handpainted cinema billboards – and then jump off at the Retiro for a stroll in the gardens. Bus number 3 is a good route for an overview of the city centre; get on at the Puerta de Toledo, then stay on past the Opera, the Puerta del Sol, the Gran Vía, and finish up in Chueca just in time for a cocktail. Bus number 5 goes from the Puerta del Sol up the Paseo de la Castellana (the one street in Madrid which you definitely won't want to stroll along) to Plaza de Castilla. This one is a good option for modern architecture fans. The number 21 heads down Pintor Rosales in the northeast of the city, sweeps through Chueca (where you could stop off for some shopping), and heads out to the bullring at Ventas, where you could have some tapas and visit the bullfighting museum.

## Car
Driving in Madrid is a nightmare and entirely unnecessary given the excellent public transport system. If you do bring a car to Madrid, park in a staffed underground car park. Cars with foreign plates or rental cars are particular targets for thieves. Parking is banned on many of the streets in the city centre; if you park illegally and get towed away, call T 91 345 00 50 to track down your car. The most central of the 30 underground municipal car parks in Madrid can be found at Plaza Santa Ana, Plaza Mayor and Plaza de España. These are all open round the clock and cost around €15 for 24 hours.

Car hire is surprisingly expensive. Check if your airline offers any special deals and search the internet for the best bargains. It costs between €30-60 per day for the cheapest car. There are often deals at weekends or for week-long car hire. Usually, drivers need to be over 21 and to have held their driving licenses for at least a year. For a list of car hire companies, see p216.

## Cycling
Madrid is not a bike-friendly city and there are no cycle lanes on the main streets; cycling in the city centre is only for the very brave. However, it can be fun to cycle around parks like the Buen Retiro or the huge Casa de Campo, where there are some cycle paths. For bike hire, see Directory p216. There's some excellent mountain biking in the Sierras around the city.

**Travel extras**

**Safety** Like most big cities, Madrid suffers from pickpockets, especially in the Puerta del Sol when you should grip hard onto your bags – just as the locals do. Prostitution is carried out very obviously on Calle Montera, behind the Telefónica building on the Gran Vía and in the Casa de Campo which might make some people uncomfortable. There are some areas which can feel a bit dark and unpleasant – around the Plaza Tirso de Molina and some parts of La Latina and Lavapiés for example – but in general, there are enough people out in the streets for tourists not to feel too threatened. The Basque organization ETA has detonated car bombs in its campaign for Basque liberation, but it´s no more likely tourists wil get caught up in terrorist activities in Madrid than it would be in other western cities, for example. For the very latest information, check out the Foreign and Commonwealth Office website on www.fco.org.uk

## Metro

Madrid's metro system is clean, safe, efficient and easy to use. Each of the 10 lines is colour-coded and numbered and you just need to know the final destination of your train to ensure you are going in the right direction. There are signs and maps everywhere. The metro is to be avoided during the rush hour, around 0800-0900 and in the evening from about 1800-2000, and during the height of summer when it gets hot and stuffy. The metro runs from about 0630 until 0100. Free metro plans are available at tourist offices, at metro stations, or online at www.ctm-madrid.es A single metro journey costs €0.95, or you can buy a Metrobús ticket from stations and tobacconists (*estancos*) for €5, valid for 10 journeys on buses or metro.

## Taxi

Madrid has more taxis than any other European city, so hailing one is never a problem. Taxis are white with a red stripe on the front doors. There are several taxi ranks, including at the Puerta de Sol or near the metro station at Opera. Prices are reasonable; a taxi from the Prado to the Palacio Real on the other side of the city will cost around €4, for example. There are supplements, however, for luggage, pets, travel after 2200 and at weekends.

## Train

Cercanías are the local trains and are useful for crossing the city. Trains shuttle every few minutes from Atocha station in the south to Chamartín in the north. They are faster and slightly cheaper than the metro. Metro tickets are not valid unless you have an *abono de transporte* which is valid on all forms of transport, but available for longer periods only.

## Walking

Madrid is a delightful city to walk around; the centre is relatively small and most of the sights are within easy walking distance of each other. It takes about 15 minutes to walk from the Prado Museum to Plaza Mayor and about another 15 minutes to walk from Plaza Mayor to the Palacio Real. It's easy to get lost – but that is half the charm. Free maps are provided by the tourist information offices and there's a good selection of better maps at most bookstores. For walking tours, see p29.

**Museums and monuments**

The following are free on the days stated: Prado, Saturday afternoon and Sunday; Museo Nacional Centro de Arte Reina Sofía, Saturday afternoon and Sunday; Museo Nacional de Artes Decoratives, Sunday; Real Academia de Bellas Artes de San Fernando, Wednesday; Museo Cerralbo, Wednesday and Sunday; Panteón de Goya, Wednesday and Sunday; Museo de América, Sunday; Museo Arqueológico Nacional, Saturday afternoon and Sunday. All Royal properties run by the Patrimonio Nacional are free to EU passport holders on Wednesday. Most museums and galleries close on Monday with a few exceptions, see the listings.

# Tours

The municipal tourist office, see p30, has a full list of sightseeing tours available and organizes its own walking tours and coach excursions to towns outside Madrid.

## Bus tours

*Juliatur*, Gran Vía 68, T 91 559 96 05, conduct tours around Madrid, including night-time tours and excursions to towns around the city. Prices vary according to the tour. *Madrid Tour*, T 902 10 1081, www.citysightseeing-spain.com, is another hop-on/hop-off service which offers three routes around Madrid. Prices are around €10; €5 for children and seniors. *Madrid-Visión*, T 91 779 18 88, www.trapsa.com/mvision, is a popular hop-on/hop-off double-decker bus with similar prices and routes to *Madrid Tour* (above). *Pullmantour*, Plaza de Oriente 8, T 91 541 18 05, offers a wide selection of tours, both within the city centre and further afield. Prices vary. See also DIY bus sightseeing tours, p24.

**Paseo del Arte voucher**

This voucher or *abono* offers entry to each of the Big Three for €7.66. It's available at ticket desks in all three museums and is valid from the year of purchase until 31 December the following year. Note that it does not include entrance to temporary exhibitions.

## Cycling tours

*Bravo Bike.com*, Av Menorca, 2 E, Las Rozas, T 91 640 12 98, book tours on T 607 448 440 or T 677 356 586 at least one day in advance, www.bravobike.com A friendly outfit that will collect you from your hotel and provide all equipment. They offer a range of bicycle tours (with multilingual guides), both in Madrid itself and around the city, including El Escorial, Segovia and La Granja, Chinchón and Aranjuez, as well as mountain biking in the Sierras for more advanced cyclists. *Esto es Madrid*, Calle Torpedero Tucumán 18, T 91 350 11 60, www.estoesmadrid.net, offer mountain biking tours in and around Madrid; includes a women-only bike tour.

## Walking tours

The municipal tourist information office on Plaza Mayor offers a vast array of walking tours, outlined in a free booklet called *Descubre Madrid*. Prices start at around €3.

# Tourist information

Tourist information offices can provide you with a basic plan of the city and a copy of *En Madrid What's On*, a pocket-sized magazine with helpful local information and listings. The main office is at Calle del Duque de Medinaceli 2, T 91 429 37 05. *Open Mon-Fri 0900-1900, Sat 0900-1300*. Other branches are at Barajas Airport, T1, T 91 305 85 56, *Mon-Fri 0800-2000, Sat 0900-1300*; Chamartín train station, Gate 16, T 91 315 99 76, *Mon-Fri 0800-2000, Sat 0900-1300*; Mercado Puerta de Toledo, Ronda de Toledo 1, T 91 364 18 76, *Mon-Fri 0900-1900, Sat 0930-1330*. The City of Madrid office is at Plaza Mayor 3, T 91 366 54 77. *Open Mon-Fri 1000-1400, Sat 1000-1500*. Pick up the free English-language monthly newspaper *InMadrid*, with plenty of bar and club listings. There is a tourist information line, T 902 100 007, and a city information line, T 010, both of which usually have English-speaking operators. There are two official websites: www.comadrid.es, run by the regional authority, and www.munimadrid.es, run by the city.

# Paseo del Prado and around

*Madrid is home to three of Europe's most important art museums –
the **Prado**, the **Reina Sofía** and the **Thyssen-Bornemisza** – all
happily located within strolling distance of each other (although only
the most fanatical art buff would consider visiting all three in a single
day). The Prado's strength is its magnificent collection of Spanish
masterpieces from the 12th to the 19th centuries, including works by
Velázquez, Zurbarán and Goya. The luminous Reina Sofía displays
works spanning the last century, including Picasso's celebrated
Guernica. The Thyssen-Bornemisza perfectly complements both
collections. It plugs the gaps left by the Prado with its vast collection of
western European art spanning eight centuries and offers a dazzling
selection of early 20th-century masters from Braque to Kandinsky to
whet your appetite for the Reina Sofía. There's a scattering of smaller
museums and curiosities a stroll away from the Big Three (known as
the Triángulo del Arte), like the **Fábrica Real de Tapices**, where the
old methods of creating tapestry have barely changed in the last few
hundred years, or the **Cibeles Fountain**, where Real Madrid fans
come to celebrate their victories.*

▸▸ *See Sleeping p115, Eating and drinking p132, Bars and clubs p159*

## ◉ Sights

---

### ★ Museo del Prado

Paseo del Prado s/n, **T** 91 330 28 00, www.museoprado.mcu.es
*Tue-Sat 0900-1900, Sun 0900-1400. €3/1.50 concessions, free Sat
afternoon. Metro Banco de España. Map 3, E1/F1, p250*

The Prado museum houses one of the world's greatest art
collections – a dazzling display of European art spanning seven
centuries. When it opened in 1819, it was one of the very first
public art museums, infused with the spirit of the Enlightenment,

and shored up by royal whim (Queen Isabel of Braganza had been impressed with the Louvre and wanted one for Spain). The collection is enormous; today, it holds several thousand works of art and has long outgrown Juan de Villanueva's severely elegant neoclassical building. A major expansion is scheduled for completion in 2005 (see box opposite). The Casón del Buen Retiro, which holds the museum's collection of 19th-century art, is currently closed for reconstruction.

Carlos I (Charles V) began the royal collection, his son Felipe II expanded it, but it was Felipe IV who turned it into the most important art collection of his age. It still reflects the idiosyncratic tastes of the kings and queens who formed it, and is uneven in parts – some major Spanish artists like Ribera or Murillo are barely featured, for example. The sheer scale can make it daunting, and it might be worth picking out some highlights or favourite painters.

● *There's little in the way of nightlife or restaurants in the rather staid area around the Prado – but the tapas bars and pavement cafés of Plaza Santa Ana are just a short walk way along C Huertas.*

### Ground floor

The collection of medieval art is thin but includes some gilded *retablos*, and the haunting murals from the Hermitage of Santa Cruz de Maderuelo (room 51c). Among the works from 15th-16th-century Flanders are Rogier van der Weyden's moving masterpiece, the *Descent from the Cross* (room 58), some sharply observed portraits by court painter Antonio Muro (originally from Utrecht), and the crowd-pleasing, nightmarish visions of Breughel the Elder (including *The Triumph of Death* in room 56a) and Heironymous Bosch (like *The Garden of Earthly Delights* in room 58). There isn't much from the Italian Renaissance, but what there is is exquisite: Fra Angelico's *Annunciation*, Raphael's *Fall on the Road to Calvary*, and a series of beautiful panels by Sandro Botticelli depicting a story from the *Decameron*. Albrecht Dürer's self-portrait in room 49 is the highlight of the collection of

### ▶ Gran Prado

Rafael Moneo's plans for the expansion of the Prado include a new administration building near the church of San Jerónimo behind the main Prado building linked by an underground tunnel. The Casón del Buen Retiro has been under renovation for several years and was due to reopen in 2002, but it's still shrouded in scaffolding and 2003 seems a more likely date. The Museo del Ejército is to be appropriated by the Prado who hope to return the works of Velázquez and Zurbarán to their original setting (see p42), but these plans have met with fierce opposition from army officials. The Prado looks set to win the day – but even so, the prospective completion date of 2005 for the reorganized collection seems increasingly unrealistic.

15th-16th-century German art, but don't miss the luminous panels depicting *Adam and Eve*. El Greco's paintings, including *Annunciation*, with their dazzling colours and surging, elongated forms, are in their own room, 61a; fans should visit Toledo; see p102. Tiziano Titian, a favourite with Carlow I (Charles V) and Felipe II, is well represented (room 61b), along with his fellow Venetian painters, Paolo Veronese and Jacopo Robusti Tintoretto.

### First floor

The excellent collection of French, Dutch and Italian paintings from the 17th and 18th centuries (including *Artemisia* by Rembrandt in room 7) may be the envy of art museums around the world, but they are still completely overshadowed by the Prado's greatest treasure, its huge collection of works by Diego Velázquez (1599-1660), court painter to Felipe IV, in room 12. The most famous paintings are gathered under the glass dome at the very centre of the building, including *Las Meninas*, the sublime portrait of the Infanta Margarita and her maids-in-waiting, and an acutely observed portrait of Felipe IV himself. The celebrated painting of *The Surrender of Breda* in room 16 and the equestrian portraits painted for the Salón de los Reinos (in the present Museo del Ejército, see p42) may one day be returned to their original setting (see box p35). There are some stark, brilliantly lit paintings by Zurbarán such as *Santa Isabel de Portugal* in room 18a; a handful of fluffy saints by Bartolomé Esteban Murillo; and some dark, intense depictions of martyrs by José de Ribera like *El Martirio de San Felipe* in room 26. Rubens is well represented, because the Flemish painter was in the service of the Habsburg court and visited Madrid several times; check out *The Three Graces* in room 9. Finally, there are a series of rooms devoted to Francisco Goya y Lucientes (1746-1828), court painter to Carlos IV, with his painting *El Tres de Mayo* in room 39. On this floor you'll find the grim works painted after the anti-French uprisings of 1808 (see p80, Malasaña), and the horrifying *Pinturas Negras* (Black Paintings): dark, hallucinatory pieces which were painted after the strange illness which left him deaf.

## Second floor

A whole wing is devoted to Goya. Before war and sickness plunged Goya into depression, his works were characterized by joyful scenes and vivid colours. The early tapestry cartoons sparkle with life, but Goya's most famous works are the mysterious *The Nude Maja* and *The Clothed Maja* in room 89a, daringly modelled, some say, on Goya's beautiful, and unconventional patron, the Duchess of Alba.

## Basement

The basement of the Prado contains the Dauphin's Treasure, a dazzling collection of jewelled Renaissance and baroque tableware and glassware, which originally belonged to Louis de Bourbon, son of Louis XIV, who gave the collection its name. It's one of the most remarkable collections of its kind in the world; a single goblet is encrusted with 23 emeralds, plus plenty of cameos and cornelians.

## ★ Museo Nacional Centro de Arte Reina Sofía

*C Santa Isabel 52, **T** 91 467 50 62, www.reinasofia.mcu.es Mon, Wed-Sat 1000-2100, Sun 1000-1430. €3.01/1.50 concessions, free Sat afternoon and Sun. Free guided visits Mon, Wed at 1700, Sat at 1100. Audioguides too. Metro Atocha. Map 2, H6, p248*

This museum is housed in a former hospital, which has been beautifully remodelled to hold the nation's collection of 20th-century art. It's a graceful, light-filled building set around a quiet, interior courtyard, with a pair of panoramic glass lifts which are almost an attraction in themselves. The second and fourth floors are devoted to the permanent exhibition and the first and third floors are used for temporary exhibitions which are usually excellent.

### Second floor

This floor traces the development of Spanish art from the turn of the 20th century to the conclusion of the Civil War in 1939. José Solana's *The Gathering at the Café del Pombo* in room 2 reflects the intensity of intellectual life in Madrid's cafés, but it was the Basques and the Catalans who were creating the most innovative work in painting and sculpture; Isidre Nonell's haunting studies of gypsies in the streets of Barcelona profoundly influenced Picasso's Blue period. At the start of the 20th century, Paris was the mecca of the art world, and Spanish artists soaked up the avant-garde art movements; Juan Gris developed his personal interpretation of Cubism (see *The Singer* in room 4) and Pau Gargallo's whiplash, wrought- iron sculptures treated space in an entirely new way. Both collaborated with Picasso, whose works are displayed in a line of galleries here. At the centre is *Guernica* in room 6, his vast, anguished response to the bombing of a Basque village during the Civil War. The Picasso galleries are flanked by galleries devoted to Joan Miró, who created a personal sign language in his colourful, abstract paintings; see *Woman* in room 15. There are some light,

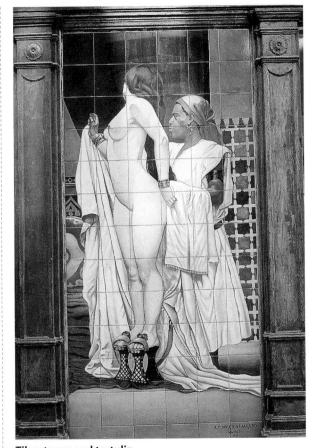

## Tiles, tapas and tertulia
*These beautifully decorated tiles welcome visitors to cafés in the Calle Espoz y Mina in Puerto del Sol.*

graceful mobile sculptures by Alexander Calder (including *Constellation* in room 9), and two rooms are devoted to Dalí's surreal, melting landscapes. Finally, there's a mixed collection of sculpture.

## Fourth floor

Spain's artistic and cultural life was mercilessly repressed in the first years of Franco's dictatorship. During the 1950s, some of the most interesting work was being done by the Basque sculptor, Jorge Oteiza, whose boxy, iron pieces inspired Equipo 57, a collective committed to exploring notions of space. There is a good collection of international artists: paintings by Sir Francis Bacon (see *Reclining Figure* in room 24), Yves Klein's trademark brilliant blue works, a tiny, serene sculpture by Henry Moore and slashed canvases by Lucio Fontana. Several galleries are devoted to the Catalan artist Antoni Tàpies, whose unsettling 'material paintings' are created from layers of 'found' objects in room 35 (see his *Seven Chairs*). Antonio López's vast sculpture *Man and Woman* in room 31 is set alongside some haunting landscapes of Madrid. The Spanish collective Equipo Crónico attacked mass culture imported from the US in their pop art-style pieces from the late 1960s and 1970s; the most recent works include a group of severely abstract sculptures from Eduardo Chillida, like *The Spirit of the Birds* in room 41.

---

## ★ Museo Thyssen-Bornemisza

Paseo del Prado 8, **T** 91 369 01 51, www.museothyssen.org
*Tue-Sun 1000-1900. €4.81/2.40 concessions. Metro Banco de España. Map 4, D11/12, p253*

When the Spanish state bought the Thyssen-Bornemisza collection in 1993, it proved a neat complement to the Prado and Reina Sofía collections. It fleshes out the collections of medieval Flemish and Italian art held at the Prado, and adds an international dimension to the 20th-century art at the Reina Sofía. Unlike the other two corners of the Triángulo del Arte, the Thyssen works from the bottom down; head to the second floor for the earliest art.

## Second floor

The Thyssen's collection of medieval art is especially strong. It opens with the luminous works of the Italian Primitives, followed by some glittering, highly decorative paintings in the International Gothic style which swept across Europe in the early 15th century. Van der Weyden's *Madonna and Child Enthroned* and Van Eyck's *Annunciation Diptych* are in room 3 and as well as Campen are among the early Dutch and Flemish masters. There are also some beautiful Renaissance portraits, including Holbein's celebrated portrait of Henry VIII and *Portrait of Giovanna Tornabuoni* by Ghirlandaio in room 5. The bold energy of the Venetian colourists (the Thyssen is particularly strong on Venetian art) is echoed in El Greco's energetic works (see his *Annunciation,* room 11) and there's a gaudy selection of sentimental 17th-century baroque art from England, Flanders and Italy. Pieces by Rubens include *The Toilet of Venus* hung beside Jan Breughel's fabulous *Garden of Eden*, room 19, and Bruggen's compelling depiction of *Esau Selling his Birthright*.

## First floor

The Thyssen's extensive collection of Dutch genre painting reveals how architecture, everyday objects and landscapes become increasingly important and would pave the way for the Golden Age of Dutch art a few decades later; one highlight is *Family Group* by Frans Hals in room 22. Two galleries are devoted to 19th-century North American art including some beautiful light-drenched pieces by John Singer Sargent. There are a couple of late Goyas, some wistful, bucolic scenes by Corot, and a small collection of Impressionist and post-Impressionist works including Degas' delightful *Swaying Dancer*, a couple of swirling Van Gogh's and Cézanne's richly textured *Portrait of a Farmer* in room 33. A gallery is devoted to the dazzling colours of the Fauvists. The undoubted highlight of this floor is the magnificent Expressionist collection, with works by Shiele, Munch, Kandinsky, Macke, Otto Dix and Max Beckmann (including Quappi in a Pink Sweater, room 39).

## Ground floor

The blazing colours and wheeling forms of the experimental artists of the early 20th century seem to leap from the walls: Picasso's splintered *Man with a Clarinet* and his *Harlequin with a Mirror* in room 45, Léger's weaving *The Staircase (second state)* in room 41, or Mondrian's obsessively geometric *New York City, New York* in room 43. These galleries are a roll-call of the biggest names in 20th-century art: Picasso, Miró, Kandinsky, Pollock (*Brown and Silver I* is in room 46), Rothko (including *Green on Maroon*, also in room 46) and Dalí are just some of the artists featured. Lichtenstein's knowing cartoonish *Woman in a Bath* in room 48, and a portrait by Sir Francis Bacon are among the most recent works.

## Paseo del Prado
*Map 2 overview*

This elegant, boulevard created in the 19th century was once the most popular place for fashionable people to take their evening *paseo*. Nowadays, its leafy calm is entirely broken by the whizzing traffic which roars on either side. At one end is the Plaza de Cibeles, a busy roundabout with flood-lit fountains and an enormous statue of the goddess Cibeles in her chariot. Real Madrid fans launch themselves at Cibeles to celebrate victories – she lost a hand in 1994 which had to be stuck back on with a special resin, and now she gets boarded up when danger looms. Just a few hundred metres away, at the other end, Neptune and his sea horses rear out of another fountain stuck in the middle of the Atocha roundabout. Neptune gets the Atlético fans.

## Real Jardín Botánico

Plaza de Murillo 2, **T** 91 420 30 17. *1000-sunset. €1.50/0.70 concessions, free to under 10s and senior citizens. Metro Atocha. Map 3, H2, p250*

These languid gardens, with their plentiful fountains and birdsong, are a cool oasis in the deadening heat of summer. The first Royal Botanical Gardens were begun to collect plants and herbs with medicinal properties. They were given this elegant new home in the 18th century and now more than 30,000 plants are on display, including the Madrone or Strawberry Tree which is now the city's symbol (see p47).

## Museo del Ejército

C Méndez Núñez 1, **T** 91 522 89 77. *Tue-Sun 1000-1400. €0.60, free on Sat. Closed Aug. Metro Banco de España. Map 3, D2, p250*

Housed in the main surviving building of the Royal Palace of the Buen Retiro, the Army Museum displays a vast collection of armour, uniforms and weaponry gathered over two centuries and dating back more than a millennium. It's a popular weekend jaunt for Madrileño dads and their kids, who seem to find the ranks of armour, pistols, swords and muskets endlessly fascinating. Miraculously, the building has preserved one of the grandest ceremonial halls of the former palace, the dazzling Salón de los Reinos, blazing with the escutcheons of the 24 kingdoms which made up Spain in the 17th century.

## Museo Nacional de Artes Decorativas

C Montalbán 12, **T** 91 532 64 99. *Tue-Fri 0930-1500, Sat-Sun, public holidays 1000-1400. €2.40/1.20, free to over-65s and on Sun. Metro Banco de España. Map 3, C1, p250*

This huge museum is stuffed with furniture, porcelain, tapestries and tiles from all over Spain. Highlights include a pair of winsome hansom cabs from the 17th-century, an elaborately tiled 18th-century Valencian kitchen and a delightful collection of 19th-century dolls' houses, complete with gilded wallpaper and chandeliers. Several galleries are devoted to ceramics and porcelain, including the shimmering platters and vases typical of Manzes.

### Museo Naval

Paseo del Prado 5, **T** 91 379 52 99. *Tue–Sun 1030–1330. Free. ID required. Metro Banco de España*   *Map 3, G1, p250*

The Naval Museum is housed in the brutally ugly Ministry of Defence building, but the galleries have been handsomely remodelled inside. The sections which deal with the Age of Discovery, when Spain ruled the seas and a great swathe of the known world, are surprisingly engrossing, with maps and models showing how the 15th- and 16th-century explorers staked their claims to the New World.

### Plaza de la Lealtad

*Metro Banco de España.*   *Map 3, D1, p250*

The creamy curves of the Ritz hotel overlook the circular garden of the Plaza de la Lealtad (Loyalty Square). The obelisk and eternal flame flickering in the middle of the garden commemorate the victims of the uprising on 2 May 1808 (see p80, Malasaña).

### ★ Parque del Retiro

C Alfonso XIII. *Metro Banco de España or Retiro.*   *Map 3, p250*

This dreamy expanse of manicured gardens, lakes, shady woods and pavilions was once the garden of the Palacio Real del Buen Retiro. The lake, or *estanque*, at the centre is flanked by ranks of columns and overlooked by a ridiculous statue of Alfonso XII; it used to be the scene of royal regattas, when galleons would set sail in mock-battles performed to entertain the court. The lake has just had a lengthy clean-up, and you can hire a row-boat or sit at a lakeside café. At the southern end of the park, take a peek at the bizarre Angel Caído (Fallen Angel), one of only three monuments in the world to Satan, caught midway in his fall from Paradise.

Ricardo Velázquez designed the elegant **Palacio de Velázquez** and **Palacio de Cristal** in 1882. The pavilions are now used for the Reina Sofía's temporary art exhibitions. The first, the red-brick Palacio de Velázquez, was encrusted with colourful tiles by Daniel Zuloaga, and the second, a feather-light, ethereal glass palace, is beautifully reflected in a little lake with a shooting fountain at its centre.

Juan de Villanueva's charming neoclassical **Observatorio Astronómico Nacional** sits on a small hill overlooking the Retiro. It still functions, although you need special permission to see the stars. Inside is a small museum containing a dusty collection of old telescopes, sundials and sextants.

### Estación Atocha
*Metro Atocha or Atocha RENFE.  Map2, H7, p249*

Atocha train station was massively expanded a decade ago when the high-speed AVE trains to Seville were inaugurated for Expo 1992. It's now a gleaming, ultra-modern complex packed with shops and restaurants. The original 19th-century station, a graceful wrought-iron and glass frame, has been turned into a tropical garden, with lofty palm trees and terrapins; perfect for a coffee on a wintry day.

**!** The nucleus of the Anthropology Museum's collection was gathered by the eccentric Dr Pedro González Velasco, who famously embalmed his daughter and could be seeing driving around in his carriage with her body propped up beside him.

### Real Fábrica de Tapices

C Fuentarrabía 2, **T** 91 434 05 50.  *Mon-Fri 1000-1400. Guided visits only, €2. Metro Menéndez Pelayo.  Map 2, H4, p248*

The vast hangings are still threaded by hand on enormous 18th-century wooden looms at these fascinating workshops. When it's time to move onto a new section, the tapestry is cranked up with a huge wooden pole and a team of puffing overalled workers pulling together on a rope. It takes about a week for one person to create just one metre square of the tapestry, and even longer for the more delicate work in silk that takes place in a separate room.

### Museo de Antropología

C Alfonso XII 68, **T** 91 530 64 18.  *Tue-Sat 1000-1930, Sun 1000-1400. €2.40. Just beyond Estación Atocha  Metro Atocha.*

The dusty Anthropology Museum contains a ragbag of artefacts gathered from around the world, particularly from former Spanish possessions like the Philippines. One room contains the bizarre corpse of an extremely tall man, 2.35 m, who sold his body to science before his death. There's also the desiccated head of a decapitated Chinese pirate and some gruesome cabinets of dusty bones.

## Sol, Huertas and Santa Ana

*The **Puerta del Sol** is the crossroads of Madrid, the meeting point of ten major roads and shopping streets. It's no beauty, but the endless flow of shoppers and commuters give it a certain brash energy. Just a few steps away is the enticing web of streets around the **Plaza Santa Ana**, which slope downhill towards the Prado museum. This engaging neighbourhood of blind alleys, leaning houses and old-fashioned shops is packed with traditional tapas bars and restaurants, many still covered in turn-of-the-20th-century tiles. It's the perfect place for a tapas, on summer weekends, the pavements*

★ **Highlights around Sol and Santa Ana**

- Tapas crawl around Plaza Santa Ana, p50
- Casa-Museo Lope de Vega, p51
- Jazz at the Café Central, p177
- Iglesia de Jesús de Medinaceli on the first Friday of the month, p55

*are crammed all night with at least as many tourists as Madrileños. There are few reminders that this neighbourhood was once home to Cervantes, Lope de Vega, Quevado and other great writers of the Golden Age, but you can visit Lope de Vega's delightful home, the* **Casa-Museo Lope de Vega***, on Calle Cervantes. On the fringes of this bohemian barrio is the decidedly un-bohemian parliament building, the* **Palacio del Congreso** *or Las Cortes, and the sweet delights of some of Madrid's oldest patisseries.*

▸▸ *See Sleeping p116, Eating and drinking p134, Bars and clubs p160*

 Sights

★ **Puerta del Sol**
*Metro Sol  Map 6, A8, P256*

Puerta del Sol is one of Madrid's main hubs, a bustling, untidy thoroughfare which marks the meeting point of several major roads and shopping streets. It's disappointingly bland and although there is a constant flow of people, they are always on their way to somewhere else. The city council has recently made things worse by ripping out all the square's benches (in a failed attempt to dislodge the immigrants who still stand around looking bored). It wasn't always this way: the Puerta del Sol used to be the most piquant neighbourhood in Madrid, the steps of the convents which once stood here were well-known gossip shops, and if you needed to find an assassin in a hurry, this was the place to come. The square's animation was legendary, then the pavement cafés were replaced with generic chain stores and fast food outlets and now there is very little to detain anybody although the 19th-century pastry shop and café, *La Mallorquina* (see p191) is well worth a visit.

The grand, pinkish building which takes up one side of the square is the former post office (now government offices) and right outside it is a plaque which marks the very centre of Spain – 'Kilometre Zero' – from which all distances are measured. This is also where Madrileños gather to bring in the New Year, traditionally eating one grape at each chime of the bell from the clock tower. The other famous landmark is the huge neon Tío Pepe sign, blazoned across the roof of the *Hotel Paris*, Madrid's very first luxury hotel. Its days of glory have long since gone and now it's a monument to 1950s kitsch.

The usual meeting point on the square is at the 'bear and the madroño tree' – the big, bronze state of Madrid's symbol which stands near the *El Corte Inglés* bookshop. No one quite knows how this unlikely pair came to symbolize the city, and the legends which now surround it are disappointingly prosaic – it seems most likely that the madroño tree shares the first part of its name with Madrid and that the region was once full of bears.

● *If you want to see what a madroño tree looks like, the council have planted several along the Calle Mayor.*

## Carrera de San Jerónimo
*Metro Sol or Sevilla.  Map 4, D10/11, p253*

This street leads down from the Puerta de Sol to the Plaza Cánovas del Castillo. It used to be part of the ceremonial route from the Palacio Real on the western side of the city to the Palacio del Buen Retiro on its eastern flank, but now it's lined with showy banks, and fancy offices. This neighbourhood is perfect for gourmets,

**Party town**
The Tío Pepe advertising dominates the skyline of the Puerta del Sol, a magnet for Madrileños on New Year's Eve when grapes are eaten at each chime of the bell from the clock tower.

particularly anyone with a sweet tooth. The most famous gourmet institution in all Madrid is *Lhardy* at Carrera de San Jerónimo 8, which was founded in 1839 by Emilio Lhardy after the French writer Prosper Mérimée (author of *Carmen*) urged him to introduce French pastries to the Spanish capital. It began as a patisserie and delicatessen with a nice little sideline in home-delivered cooked meals, but the business took off so rapidly that a restaurant was added upstairs. Its elegant panelled ooms provided the perfect setting for illicit love affairs among the upper classes, including Isabel II herself (a nymphomaniac, by all accounts).

---

## ★ Plaza Santa Ana
*Metro Antón Martín. Map4, E8/9, p253*

This square, flanked by bars, restaurants, theatres and hotels, has been the heart of the Barrio de los Literatos (see p51) for centuries. It's been overhauled a dozen times and is currently shrouded in scaffolding from its latest incarnation, which looks set to continue Madrid's infuriating tradition of creating banal public squares. Although not especially pretty, the square's undoubted charm lies in its vibrancy and constant animation; the pavements are lined with terraces from the dozens of tapas bars, many of which are filled with turn-of-the-20th-century fittings, and it's one of the most popular places in Madrid for the *tapeo* (going from tapas bar to tapas bar). On summer nights, the pavements are dense with visitors (it's hugely popular with tourists, especially those on the Hemingway trail), locals walking their dogs, and elderly Madrileños sitting on benches watching the world go by. It's flanked by the **Teatro Española** where audiences baited Lorca with calls of 'queer' and 'whore' during the première of *Yerma* in 1934. Opposite the theatre is the belle époque-style *Gran Hotel Victoria*, a favourite with bullfighters, which has a plaque to Manolete, perhaps the most famous *torero* of all time.

## ▶ Literary living

The neighbourhood around Santa Ana and Calle Huertas has long been associated with some of Spain's most famous writers and intellectuals and it's still sometimes called El Barrio de los Literatos. The street names recall some of the most celebrated names of the Golden Age, like Lope de Vega, play-wright, poet and satirist, and Cervantes, author of *Don Quixote*, who lived just a few doors apart and hated each other with a passion. Francisco de Quevedo, who also has a street named after him, was the author of *La Vida del*

*Buscón* (The Swindler), a classic picaresque novel which relates the adventures of Don Pablo (the swindler of the title) with malicious brilliance. The late 19th century marked another flowering of literature and ideas which is sometimes called the Silver Age. The cafés of Santa Ana hummed with new ideas expressed in fervent discussions (*tertulias*). Sadly, almost all the famous literary cafés – like the *Fontana de Oro*, which was chronicled by Pérez Galdós in his historical novel *La Fontana de Oro* – have disappeared.

## Casa-Museo Lope de Vega

C Cervantes 11, **T** 91 429 92 16. *Tue-Fri 0930-1400, Sat 1000-1400, closed Sat, Sun, Aug, holidays. Tour by guided visit only (in Spanish) €2/1.50 for concessions. Metro Antón Martín. Map 4, E10, p253*

Félix Lope de Vega (1562-1635) was one of the most prolific and charismatic writers of Madrid's Golden Age. He wrote thousands of plays, poems and satire, poked fun at all his rivals (especially Cervantes) and still found time to lead a stormy love life which scandalized and enthralled Spanish society. Lope de Vega bought this house in 1610 and lived here until his death in 1635; he loved his new home, 'my little house, my tranquillity, my little plot, my study' he wrote not long after moving in, and it is now a delightfully intimate and serene museum. The peaceful, enclosed garden was Lope de Vega's pride and joy and has been beautifully restored and filled with period furniture to look much as it would have when sat here and read five centuries ago (the staff are happy to let visitors do the same now). Lope de Vega's bedroom and book-lined study are on the first floor, and a small grille in the bedroom overlooks the charming private chapel where Lope de Vega could watch services from his bed when he became ill towards the end of his life. Another curiosity is the curtained-off platform area where the women of the house would sit and sew on floor cushions, in the Moorish style.

● *Lope de Vega fared better than his arch-rival Cervantes, whose former home – just up the street at the corner of Calle Léon and Calle Cervantes – was demolished in the early 19th century despite a loud chorus of public outrage. The site is now marked with a simple plaque.*

---

### Calle de las Huertas
*Metro Antón Martín.* Map 4, F10/11, p253

The main business of sloping down Calle de las Huertas, like most streets in this neighbourhood, has traditionally been entertainment: once it was brothels, but now it's lined with lively bars, restaurants, and jazz cafés. A couple of incongruously respectable monuments are tucked away, neither open to the public, which might be worth a glance.

The forbidding, walled complex of the **Convento de las Trinitarias Descalzas** (not open to visitors) was founded in 1612 and, by curious coincidence, the daughters of Lope de Vega and Cervantes were both nuns here. Cervantes was buried here, but, in inimitable Madrileño fashion, his bones – like the bones of most of the city's most celebrated citizens – have been lost.

It is not the bustle of a busy people; it is the vivacity of cheerful persons, a carnival-like joy, a restless idleness, a feverish overflow of pleasure that takes hold of you and makes you want to go round and round the square without leaving it

*Italian writer, Edmondo de Amicis, on the Puerta del Sol*

**Madrid**

### ▶ Street theatre

At the height of Madrid's Golden Age in the 16th and 17th centuries, this neighbourhood used to be densely clustered with theatres, its streets teeming with actors, aristocrats with a taste for the low life and a motley crew of traders, card sharps and whores from the nearby brothels. Plays were once staged in *corrales* (courtyards), and the name was echoed in the purpose-built theatres which were erected in the streets around the Plaza Santa Ana – the long-demolished Corral de Príncipe and the Corral de Cruz. The infamously rowdy audiences were more than happy to lynch the playwright if they didn't like the way the drama was heading – frightened authors often changed the endings midway through performances rather than face the outrage.

### Calle Atocha and Cine Doré
*Metro Antón Martín and Atocha. Map 4, G9/10, p253*

Calle Atocha is one of the main road arteries of central Madrid: noisy, slightly seedy and lined with cheap *pensiones* and *hostales*. Just off Plaza Antón Martín at the top of the hill is Madrid's most delightful cinema, the winsome, art deco Cine Doré which is now the Filmoteca Nacional (see p172). It has a very pretty café and terrace, too. Cine Doré also made an appearance in the recent Pedro Almodóvar movie *Hable con ella* (Talk to her). Love-struck Benigno visits the cinema to see a silent movie having adopted the interests of his comatosed "girlfriend".

● *Downhill, the site of the printing shop at C Atocha 87, where the first part of Cervantes' famous novel* Don Quixote *was published, is slated to become a museum dedicated to the writer.*

## Palacio del Congreso (Las Cortes)

Plaza de las Cortes, C San Jerónimo, **T** 91 390 65 25. *Guided tours about every 30 mins Sat 1000-1300, closed Aug, photo ID required. Free. Metro Banco de España or Sevilla. Map 4, D11, p253*

Spain's government is housed in one of the dullest parliament buildings in Europe, a dreary greyish neoclassical edifice guarded by a pair of bronze lions. Inside, things liven up and it looks much more suited for the serious business of governing the country, with plenty of 19th-century plush red velvet, stained glass and enormous chandeliers. Back in 1981, Spain's fledgling democracy came under threat when Colonel Tejero and his troops stormed the main assembly hall, firing off shots (the bullet holes can still be seen, but you have to ask discreetly) and took the Cortes hostage for more than 24 hours. The nation, listening to the drama on the radio, held its breath, but democracy finally won out when leaders of all political parties banded together in a mass demonstration through the streets of Madrid.

## Iglesia Jesús de Medinaceli

Plaza de Jesús. *Metro Antón Martín. Map 4, E11, p253*

On the first Friday of each month you'll stumble across extraordinary queues of people snaking endlessly around the streets around the Plaza de Jesús. Some queue all night and, very occasionally, you'll see a particularly devout old lady inching along on her knees. The object of their patient vigil is a 16th-century statue of Jesús de Medinaceli, held in the otherwise ugly church of the same name which overlooks the Plaza de Jesús. According to legend, the statue was stolen by pirates who demanded its weight in gold as ransom. But when the exchange took place and the statue was placed on the scales, it was miraculously found to weigh only as much as a single coin. The church itself replaced an earlier chapel that was notorious for its eleven o'clock masses on

## ★ Best

**Highlights around the Plaza Mayor**

- Finding La Calderona's balcony on the Plaza Mayor, p59
- Buying cakes at the Convento de las Carboneras, p58
- Seeing the Reliquario in the Convento de la Encarnación, p66
- Visiting the Palacio Real, p62
- An evening at the Teatro Real, see p65

Sundays, which were attended by the greatest actresses of the Golden Age, all dressed in their glittering best.

● *Just across the small square – not much more than a widening in the street – is one of Madrid's most emblematic tiled bars, the Taberna Las Dolores (see p137).*

# Plaza Mayor and Los Austrias

*The Plaza Mayor is the grandest square in all Madrid, completely enclosed, and surrounded by elegant arcades. The Madrileños have all but abandoned it to tourists, but it's still a handsome spot for a coffee out on the terrace. The area around it is known as* **Habsburg Madrid***, or Madrid of the Austrias, and the winding streets and passages are sprinkled with old palaces and monasteries, tiny churches and traditional shops selling handmade guitars, religious goods, or fine wines. Its proximity to the royal palace has meant that this neighbourhood has always been pretty fancy – at least until the posh families moved out to the grand new avenues of Salamanca a century or so ago – and the restaurants and smart tapas bars are a cut above the workaday places in other parts of the city. Even the convents were established for blue-blooded nuns and are stuffed with treasures; a pair of them have now opened their doors to visitors. The Moorish fortress did service as a royal palace for centuries, but the Bourbons wanted something altogether grander and built the present, enormous* **Palacio Real** *which spreads flamboyantly across*

*the western side of the city, surrounded with manicured gardens like
the **Campo del Moro**, elegant squares like the **Plaza de Oriente**
and Madrid's celebrated opera house, the **Teatro Real**.*

▸▸ *See Sleeping p121, Eating and drinking p138, Bars and clubs p162*

# ◉ Sights

---

## ★ Plaza Mayor
*Metro Sol.  Map 6, B4, p256*

The Plaza Mayor is vast, a huge cobbled expanse surrounded by
elegant arcades and tall mansions topped with steep slate roofs.
When it's bright and sunny, it's packed with terrace cafés, souvenir
shops and sun-worshipping tourists; the only time you might catch
a Madrileño here is on a Sunday morning when a stamp and coin
market is held under the arcades.

The square was built by Juan Gómez de Mora to designs by
Felipe II's favourite architect, Juan de Herrera. This was the
ceremonial centre of Madrid, a magnificent backdrop for
coronations, executions, markets, bullfights and fiestas. It is riddled
with the subterranean torture chambers of the Inquisition, who
used the square for *autos-da-fé* – the trial of suspected heretics.
In just one day in 1680, they tried 118 prisoners here and burned
21 of them alive. Before the square was built, a market was
traditionally held in front of the **Casa de la Panadería**, the old
bakery, which is now the most eye-catching building on the
square. It was repainted in 1992 by Carlos Franco who covered it
with a hippy-trippy fresco of floating nymphs.

Arched passages lead off to some of the most important streets
of 17th-century Madrid – Calle Toledo, Calle Mayor, and Calle
Segovia – as well as several which still echo the trades which were
once carried out here, like Calle Cuchilleros, the Street of the Knife-
Sharpeners, which incorporates part of the old city walls. This is

where you'll find the traditional *mesones* (inns), which grew up to cater to merchants and travellers arriving at the city gates. *Casa Botín* (see p139) opened in the 16th century and claims to be the oldest restaurant in the world.

## Mercado de San Miguel
*Metro Sol or Opera.  Map 6, C2, p256*

Right next to the Plaza Mayor is Madrid's prettiest covered market, an airy glass and wrought-iron pavilion designed by a pupil of Gustave Eiffel. It's a listed building, but is still open for fresh fish, meat, vegetables and fruit (see p192). There are several excellent upmarket tapas bars around the market (see p141) – a better bet than most of the brash, touristy ones in the Plaza Mayor.

## Plaza de la Villa
*Metro Sol.  Map 6, C1, p256*

This small, austerely beautiful square just off Calle Mayor is one of the oldest in Madrid. The grandest building is the **Casa de la Villa** (City Hall), which was begun in 1640 to plans drawn up by Juan Gómez de Moro. Until then, the city was small enough to be managed with the odd council meeting held in a local church. By 1640, it was felt that something a little more imposing was in order for what was, after all, the capital of an empire. The interior can be visited as part of the guided tours run by the city council (see p28), but there's nothing especially interesting to see besides the plush Salón de Sesiones where city matters are deliberated in a whirl of velvet and gilt. Opposite the Casa de la Villa is the **Torre de los Lujanes**, the oldest secular building in Madrid, although it's been restored almost beyond recognition. At the corner of tiny Calle del Codo, you can just make out a Moorish archway incorporated into the walls. If you duck down this little alley, you can pick up some cakes at the **Convento de las Carboneras**, see Shopping, p193.

### La Calderona's Balcony

The king and his entourage would stand on the balcony of the Casa de la Panadería during official celebrations, and citizens could chart the rise and fall of courtiers by their proximity to the king. One day, Felipe IV went too far and stood flanked on one side by his wife and on the other by his lover, a beautiful actress known as La Calderona. The queen was furious and took the actress by the hair and dragged her down to the square for a thrashing. The king ordered that a special balcony be built – you can see it hidden in the only archway onto the square which doesn't lead into a passage, right opposite the Casa de la Panadería – so that he could see his lover without upsetting his queen.

The handsome 16th-century palace which stands beyond the Casa de la Villa and closes off the square was home to Cardenal Cisneros, founder of the famous university in Alcalá (see p111). Now Madrid's Mayor, José María Alvarez del Manzano, lives here. In the centre of the Plaza de la Villa is a statue to Don Alvaro de Bazán, who was appointed leader of the Armada which was sent to fight the English, but died, perhaps fortunately, just 10 days before the expedition set off. At least he never had to discover what a misnomer 'Invincible Armada' would turn out to be.

### Calle Arenal
*Metro Sol or Opera. Map 4, C5, p252*

Calle Arenal was one of the main processional routes of Habsburg Madrid, lined with convents, palaces and churches. Now it's mainly a shopping street, with a smattering of bars, cafés and clubs. The Iglesia de San Ginés is a gloomy 17th-century church which reeks of incense, run by the shadowy, ultra-reactionary Opus Dei. There's a version of El Greco's *Expulsion from the Temple* in a small side chapel, but it's only open during services.

● *Down the passage close to the church is Madrid's best-known chocolatería (Chocolatería San Ginés, see p142) – the perfect place for churros con chocolate after a night on the tiles.*

---

★ **Monasterio de las Descalzas Reales**
Plaza de las Descalzas Reales 3, **T** 91 454 88 00. *Guided tour only (usually in Spanish) Tue-Thu, Sat 1030-1245, 1600-1745, Fri 1030-1245, Sun and holidays 1100-1330. €4.81/3.91 concessions. Free to EU passport holders on Wed. A combined ticket with the Convento de la Encarnación is available (see below, p66). Metro Sol or Opera.*
*Map 4, B5/6, p252*

This monastery was founded by Juana of Austria, daughter of Charles V (Carlos I of Spain), who was born here in its former incarnation as a royal palace. Widowed at the age of 19, she established this convent for aristocratic nuns and widows. Thanks to its royal connections, it became one of the richest religious institutions in the kingdom, crammed with paintings, tapestries and ornaments – although most were later sold when the convent fell on hard times. There is still a community of 23 nuns here, who care for the pretty kitchen gardens and orchard which can be glimpsed from the windows.

The guided tour begins with the opulent main staircase, thickly covered in *trompe l'oeil*, including a delightful one of Felipe IV and his family gathered on a balcony. At the top of the stairs, the upper gallery of the cloister is surrounded with elaborate chapels endowed by the illustrious families of nuns entering the convent, and a collection of doll-like baby Jesuses in glass cases. The gloomy choir hall (closed during services) is panelled in dark wood with candelabras in the shape of arms sprouting out surreally from the walls. The highlight of the convent is the remarkable collection of tapestries, particularly a 17th-century series called the *Triumph of*

**Madrid according to Hemingway**
*There are no mañanas in Madrid until the night has been killed off with vibrant revelry.*

*the Eucharist* which was designed by Rubens and woven in Brussels. This is where you'll find the only mirror in the whole convent, used to show off the sketch on the back of one of the tapestries. Downstairs is a recreation of a cell, complete with the spiked sandals and knotted rope which the nuns used to mortify their flesh, and some painting galleries; most are copies but the nuns have managed to hang on to a Titian.

---

## ★ Palacio Real

C Bailén s/n, **T** 91 542 00 59. *Mon-Sat 0930-1700, Sun and public holidays 0900-1400. €5.95, €6.90 with guided tour in English/€3 concessions. Free to EU passport holders on Wed. Metro Opera. Map 4, B1/C1, p252*

The Moors built their fortress on this cliff edge overlooking the Manzanares River. Over the centuries, monarchs tacked bits onto the *alcázar* to make a higgledy-piggledy royal palace that stood here until a fire destroyed it in 1734. Felipe V saw an opportunity to create something altogether grander, and commissioned the most prestigious architects of the day to create this monumental pile. Built on a staggering scale – thankfully, earlier plans for a palace four times the size of the current one were rejected – it's undoubtedly imposing, but it's no surprise that Juan Carlos I and his family have chosen to live in the more modest surroundings of the Palacio de Zarzuela on the outskirts of Madrid. The Royal Palace is still used for official functions and can be closed at short notice – if two flags are flying instead of just one, the King is at home and you won't be allowed in.Francisco Sabatini's icy staircase of pale marble leads up to the main floor, topped with a ceiling fresco depicting the *Triumph of Religion and the Church*. The **Salón de los Alabarderos** (Hall of the Halbardiers) boasts a magnificent ceiling fresco by the Venetian painter, Tiepolo, who came to Madrid at the age of 62 – some say to follow a young temptress, but this is almost certainly just a story to spice up a dull, blameless life. Carlos III was the first monarch to live in the palace and his apartments follow each other in dizzying succession. The ballroom, known as the **Hall of Columns**, swirls with gilt, crystal, cupids and thick, golden garlands. Traditionally, this is where Spanish monarchs would ceremoniously wash the feet of 25 beggars before the court, feeding them a sumptuous banquet afterwards in an annual ceremony. The most magnificent room in the palace is the **Throne Room**, finished in 1772, and densely upholstered in deep red velvet and gold, with Tiepolo's last masterpiece, *The Majesty of the Spanish Monarchy*, spreading dramatically across the vast ceiling. Tiepolo's rival, the younger and more ambitious German-born painter Antón Rafael Mengs, designed the dazzling, rococo **Gasparini Suite**, which was used as the king's dressing room. Most of the paintings are copies – the originals are exhibited at the Prado. One of the most eye-popping rooms is the **Porcelain Room**, encrusted with 134 oriental porcelain panels and silk hangings. The **Gala Dining Room** was created from three rooms by order of Alfonso XIII; possibly the only person deluded enough to think that the palace wasn't big enough, and the last king to use the palace as his residence. He had a special cinema built, and would spend Sunday afternoons here with his family. Other highlights include the exceptional collection of musical instruments in the Stradivarius room – some dating back to the 17th century, many with exquisite decorative detail.

● *Across the square, the Royal Pharmacy has a recreated 19th-century pharmacy complete with porcelain jars and fittings.*

---

## Campo del Moro

Parque-Jardín El Campo del Moro, Paseo Virgen del Puerto s/n.
*Mon-Sat 1000-1800, Sun and public holidays 0900-1800. Free.
Map 2, F11, p248*

The expansive palace gardens of the Campo del Moro spread down-hill to the Manzanares River, but you'll have to walk all the way

**Fit for kings**
*The Palacio Real, seat of the Spanish sovereign since the 18th century, as viewed through the wrought iron gates that fence in this memorial to monarchic opulence courtesy of Felipe V.*

around to the entrance on the Paseo Virgen del Puerto to get in. They are very peaceful and offer spectacular views up to the palace.

● *Equally lovely and more accessible are the Jardines del Sabatini to the north of the palace, which are very small but beautifully laid out with fountains and shady paths.*

## Plaza de Oriente
*Metro Opera. Map 4, C2, p252*

This half-moon shaped square, with its manicured gardens, statues and tranquil air is surrounded with elegant terrace cafés. It was commissioned by Joseph Bonaparte, Napoleon's brother, who was given the nickname El Rey de Plazuelas for his habit of knocking down jumbles of old buildings and replacing them with public squares. This was his first, but dozens followed. The equestrian statue of Felipe IV at the centre was built in 1640 and was moved here from the Retiro Gardens. Its construction posed problems for its sculptor, Petro Tacca, who apparently got some tips from Galileo on how to balance the horse and so made the back from solid bronze and kept the front hollow. At *El Ajibe*, the subterranean cocktail bar of the *Café de Oriente*, you can peer at the remnants of the Moorish city walls through the perspex floor (see p142).

## Teatro Real
Plaza de Oriente s/n, **T** 91 516 06 60. *Guided visits Tue-Fri at 1300, Sat, Sun and public holidays 1130-1330. Closed Aug. €3. For box office information, see p173. Metro Opera. Map 4, C3, p252*

Madrid's grand opera house was begun in 1818, and finished in 1850, just in time for Isabel II's 20th-birthday celebrations. This is where the Madrileños were introduced to the works of Verdi, Wagner and Stravinsky, along with daring new ballets by Diaghilev and the Ballet Russe. But the theatre was closed in 1925 and only finally reopened in 1997 after a massive facelift which included the addition of state-of-the-art technology. Seat prices are surprisingly good value in comparison with the UK and Madrileños still dress up in their finery to make a night out seem a very grand occasion.

## Convento de la Encarnación

Plaza de la Encarnación 1, **T** 91 454 88 00. *Guided tour only (Spanish, 20 mins) Tue-Thu, Sat 1030-1245, 1600-1745, Fri 1030-1245, Sun and holidays 1100-1345. €3.50/2.75 concessions. Combined ticket with Monasterio de las Descalzas Reales (see p60) €6/5 concessions. Metro Opera.* Map 4, B2, p252

Just to the north of the Plaza de Oriente, this small convent opened its doors to the public in the 1980s. Like other religious institutions, it has had to find new ways of funding itself under Spain's new democratic regime. The convent was commissioned by Margaret of Austria, consort to Felipe II, and was once connected to the *Alcázar* (which preceded the present Palacio Real) by a long corridor. It looks modest enough on the outside, but parts of the predominantly baroque interior are still fit for kings.

The guided tour visits 10 rooms, beginning with a series of galleries full of minor paintings and sculptures, although there's a luminous St John the Baptist by José Ribera. The highlight of the tour is the final room, the Reliquario. This subterranean, dimly lit room is lined with cabinets stuffed with the relics of thousands of saints: nails, skulls, hair, crumbling bones, and phials of blood all wrapped in garlands and displayed in intricate cases. Madrid's most famous relic is housed here, a tiny flask containing the blood of San Pantaleón which miraculously liquefies each year on the day of his martyrdom, 27 July. According to legend, if it liquefies at any other time, the country is in danger.

### ▶ Our Lady of the Almudena

Just around the corner from Madrid's cathedral on Calle Mayor is a stretch of wall with a statue of the Virgin of the Almudena (or granary) set up in a small niche. The story goes that the statue was brought to Spain by St James, and hidden here by a devout blacksmith during the ninth century when the Arabs conquered the region. After Alfonso XIII reconquered the city in 1085, he began to search for the statue. A woman promised to give up her life if it could be found, and the city walls promptly tumbled down on top of her, killing her outright, but revealing the statue. The present Virgin is a copy of one which went missing in the 16th century and has never been found – a shortage of women with an inclination for martyrdom, perhaps – but she still has a popular following and her statue is constantly surrounded by flowers.

### Catedral de Nuestra Señora de la Almudena
C Bailén, **T** 91 542 22 00. *Mon-Sat 1000-1330, 1800-2000, Sun 1000-1400, 1800-2045. Free. Mass is held daily at 1000 and 1200, Sun 1030, 1200, 1800 and 1900. Metro Opera. Map 4, D1, p252*

This huge concrete lump is Madrid's first cathedral. Right up until 1993, when it was opened amid much pomp and ceremony (and a shower of confetti made with shredded telephone directories) by Pope John Paul II, Madrid was part of the diocese of Toledo and had no cathedral to call its own. Plans for converting the former church of Our Lady of the Almudena into a cathedral were drawn up in the 1870s, but, despite more than a century of work, the finished product is profoundly banal. Much more atmospheric is the crypt (entrance around the corner on Calle Mayor), which was the first part to be completed, and has a creepy charm of its own.

# La Latina and Lavapiés

*The traditionally working-class neighbourhoods of La Latina and Lavapiés spread steeply downhill towards the Manzanares River. Known as los barrios bajos (or low neighbourhoods; see p87) they have traditionally been home to Madrid's poorest workers, smelliest industries and most desperate immigrants. This was where the slaughter houses and cigarette factories were located, and where huge, filthy tenement buildings were thrown up in the great industrial surge of the 19th century. The workers were a tough-talking, flashy dressing crowd, usually described as the Madrileño equivalent of cockneys. The latest wave of immigrants are more likely to be from North Africa, South America, Korea or China than Andalucía or Galicia, and the sinuous sounds of Arabic pop songs or Dominican salsa tunes regularly float above the rooftops. La Latina and Lavapiés are rapidly becoming Madrid's most multicultural neighbourhoods, and young artists are also moving in to add to the mix, bringing trendy bars, cafés and vintage clothes stores in their wake. The Sunday morning flea market El Rastro is a classic: follow it in true Madrileño style with a tapas crawl around the local bars.*

▶▶ *See Sleeping p123, Eating and drinking p143, Bars and clubs p163*

## ◉ Sights

### Plaza de la Paja
*Metro La Latina. Map 4, F2, p252*

Plaza de la Paja was once the most important square of medieval Madrid. Until recently, it was sadly neglected. However, newly spruced up, it has become one of the prettiest in Madrid, and the best example of the neighbourhood's continuing regeneration. Cut off from traffic, and scattered with a few trees and some benches, it is overlooked by the handsome Church of San Andrés

**★ Best**

**Highlights in La Latina and Lavapiés**

- Museo San Isidro, p69
- Rastro flea market, p74
- A drink on the buzzy Plaza de la Paja, p68
- Zarzuela performance at La Corrala, p178
- Tapas crawl around Cava Baja, p70

and ringed with restored 19th-century palaces. Some of Madrid's hippest bars have opened their designer doors and, on summer evenings, it teems with Madrid's fashionable youth.

The Plaza de la Paja is linked to the Plaza de la Humilladero, Plaza de San Andrés and Plaza de los Moros, which all form one large, pedestrian space. This is the place to come after the Rastro, see p74, when everyone spills out of the surrounding tapas bars, kids run around with their footballs, and musicians play their bongos and guitars out in the sunshine.

### Museo de San Isidro

Plaza San Andrés 2, **T** 91 366 7415, www.munimadrid.es/museo
sanisidro/ *Tue-Fri 0930-2000 (1430 in Aug), Sat-Sun 1000-1400. Free. Explanations in Spanish only, but there is a small guidebook in English available. Metro La Latina or Tirso de Molina. Map 4, G2/3, p252*

This is one of the newest city museums, dedicated to Madrid's patron saint, San Isidro, and housed in an immaculate former palace which has been completely rebuilt by the city council. According to legend, this was the house of San Isidro's masters, the Vargas family, and it was here that Isidro and his equally saintly wife, Santa María de la Cabeza once lived. Countless miracles have been attributed to the saintly duo, but one of the most celebrated is the story of their drowned child, who fell down the well. The couple prayed and prayed and finally the well filled up and overflowed, disgorging their son, who was found to be perfectly fine. This very same well (honestly) has been incorporated into the building, along with the 17th-century Capilla de San Isidro, given a layer of baroque frilliness in the 1790s, which is where the saint supposedly died. A section of the museum is devoted exclusively to the life and times of San Isidro and Santa María.

Much of the rest of the museum is devoted to a general overview of the city's history and most of the archaelogical findings formerly stored in the municipal museum have been moved to these larger, more modern surroundings. The collection still looks woefully thin, though. Altogether more attractive is the little Renaissance courtyard, with its columns, fountains and sculptures, and the charming garden (Jardín Arqueobotánico) which has examples of some of the trees to be found in medieval Madrid. The temporary exhibitions are also excellent.

### Iglesia de San Andrés and the Capilla del Obispo

Plaza de San Andrés, **T** 91 365 48 71. *Open for mass only. Metro La Latina. Map 4, F3/G3, p252*

This church was almost completely destroyed in the Civil War, and contains nothing of much interest to the visitor. The adjoining Capilla del Obispo is generally considered to be the loveliest chapel in Madrid, a Renaissance gem which has been under restoration for years. It opened in 2000 for a couple of days to everyone's delight and then mysteriously closed. Sadly, there are no plans to reopen.

### Cava Baja

*Metro La Latina. Map 4, F4/G3, p252*

Cava Baja (and the streets which feed into it) is one of the best areas in Madrid for tapas, with plenty of traditional taverns, and the odd flamenco bar. It's especially good for the obligatory post-Rastro drink.

## Catedral de San Isidro

C Toledo 37–39, **T** 91 369 2310. *Mon-Sat 0830-1230, 1830-2030, Sun and holidays 0900-1400, 1730-2030. Free.  Metro La Latina.*
*Map 6, F4, p256*

This enormous twin-towered baroque church was once the headquarters of the Jesuits in Madrid until their expulsion from Spain in 1767. The church was promptly altered to expunge all trace of the austere Jesuit style, the frothy Churrigueresque façade was added, and it was rededicated to San Isidro who had been canonized in 1622. The remains of San Isidro and his wife Santa María de la Cabeza were moved here from the chapel in the Church of San Andrés (to the fury of the local priest) and it served as the Madrileño cathedral until the Catedral de Nuestra Señora de la Almudena (see box, p67) was completed in 1993.

## Basílica de San Francisco el Grande

Plaza de San Francisco, **T** 91 365 3800. *Summer Tue-Sat 1100-1300, 1700-2000, winter 1100-1300, 1600-1900. Guided tours only, in Spanish. €1. Metro La Latina.  Map 4, H1, p252*

Larger, grander and even gloomier than the Catedral de San Isidro, the Basílica de San Francisco el Grande lives up to its name with a massive dome spanning more than 30 m. It was built between 1762 and 1784 on the ruins of a hermitage supposedly founded by Saint Francis himself, but, after the state seized the church properties in the 1830s, it briefly became barracks. Then in 1869 the church was converted into a national pantheon and the bones of some of Madrid's most famous writers were brought here, only to be returned to their original resting places a few years later. It's in the middle of a lengthy restoration project and much of it is wrapped up in scaffolding and nets. Look out for Goya's early painting of San Bernadino de Siena in the chapel dedicated to the saint.

**Glazed grandeur**
*From decorative domes and ornate ironwork, to fanciful ornamental tiles, Madrileños refuse to be outdone by Barcelona in their architectural flourishes.*

MONTES ALVAREDO

## Puerta de Toledo
*Metro Puerta de Toledo. Map 2, H2, p248*

This pompous gateway was erected in 1817 as a celebration of
Fernando VI's return to the throne after Joseph Bonaparte's brief
government. Equally unattractive is the Mercado de Toledo, a
modern development just off the roundabout, which houses an
assortment of antique and craft shops; it has never really taken off
(the disgruntled shopkeepers blame the city council for advertising
it so poorly) and is usually deserted. There are some excellent
vintage clothes stores on Calle Mira el Río Alta and Calle el Río Baja
just to the northeast. On Calle de la Paloma you'll find the lovely
neo-Mudéjar Iglesia de la Virgen de la Paloma, the focus of a
delightful pilgrimage and festival in early August (see p181).

## ★ El Rastro
C Ribera de Curtidores. *Sun mornings. Metro Tirso de Molina or
Puerta de Toledo. Map 2, H3, p248*

Madrid's famous flea market takes place every Sunday morning.
Stalls wind all the way up Calle Ribera de Curtidores and sell
everything from tacky clothes and souvenirs to leather goods,
underwear, arts and crafts and kites. The street name means
Tanner's Alley and recalls the pungent trades which took place
down here out of sight (and smell) of the smart neighbourhoods
at the top of the hill. 'Rastro' refers to the sticky trail of blood left
when the meat carcasses were hauled through the streets. The
neighbourhood is still a little shabby and run-down, although it's
in the process of regeneration and half the streets seem to have
been dug up, but the leather trade is now a thing of the past. The
surrounding shops are mainly devoted to antiques and bric-a-brac,
although you'll still find plenty of leather goods here too. Most
shops are open all week, including Sunday mornings, but the days
of a bargain are long gone. Watch out for your bags as the Rastro is

notorious for pickpockets. The atmosphere is wonderful, and carries on long after the stall-holders have packed up, when everyone heads to the surrounding bars for some tapas and a well-earned cold beer.

---

## La Corrala
Corner of C Mesón de Paredes and C Tribulete. *Metro Lavapiés.*

Most of the tenement buildings thrown up in the late 18th and early 19th centuries to provide homes for the workers in the surrounding factories and slaughterhouses have been destroyed; this is a lone survivor, which dates back to 1790. It's been given a lick of ochre paint and has undergone several restorations since the city authorities took it over in 1981, although inhabitants still complain of cracked ceilings and damp walls. The name *corrales* was given to these buildings because they were usually set around a communal courtyard (*corral*), where families would have to come to collect their water. The original courtyard has now disappeared but the square in front of the Corrala is sometimes used for traditional *zarzuela* performances in summer (see the tourist information offices for details). Don't miss it if you get the chance.

---

## Fábrica de Tabacos
C de Embajadores. *Metro Lavapiés. Map 2, H4, p248*

At the height of its production, the enormous Royal Tobacco Factory employed 3,000 women, the original Carmens, sharp-tongued beauties who were as famous for their solidarity as they were for their feistiness. They formed a powerful union and fought for an improvement in working conditions, including the establishment of schools, nurseries and pensions. By the early 20th century, mechanization had taken its toll, and the once-grand factory now stands forlorn and empty.

**★ Highlights around Gran Vía**

**Best**

- Museo Cerralbo, p78
- Museo Panteón de Goya, p82
- Real Academia de Bellas Artes de San Fernando, p77
- Museo Municipal, p79
- Cable car over to the Casa de Campo, p82

● *Head west from the Plaza San Andrés down Calle Don Pedro for Las Vistillas, a small neighbourhood of bars and cafés on top of a hill, which offers spectacular views of the sun setting over the distant sierras. During the* Fiesta de San Isidro *(see Festivals and events, p181), it's full of bands, stalls selling chocolate-dipped churros and picnicking families.*

# Gran Vía, Chueca and Malasaña

*The broad sweep of the **Gran Vía** was created at the dawn of a new age, wide enough for motor cars and lined with the city's first skyscrapers and cinemas (many of which preserve the old tradition of using handpainted billboards). Now a busy, traffic-clogged shopping street, it's looking a bit down-at-heel, but its brash, larger-than-life appeal still lingers. To the north of the Gran Vía are two formerly rundown neighbourhoods which have become the focal point of the city's heady nightlife: Chueca and Malasaña, which have both been dramatically cleaned up in the last decade. **Chueca** is the focal point of Madrid's gay community and **Malasaña** has a youthful, bohemian edge, but both are packed with some of the city's best cafés, most fashionable clubs and trendiest shopping. The **Parque del Oeste** runs along the northwest of the city; this is where the cable car leaves for the wild expanse of the **Casa de Campo** (with its zoo and funpark) and where you'll find the path to Goya's beautiful pantheon.*

▶▶ *See Sleeping p124, Eating and drinking p148, Bars and clubs p165*

# ◉ Sights

### Calle Alcalá and Círculo de Bellas Artes
C Alcalá 42, **T** 91 360 5400. *Exhibitions Tue-Fri 1700-2100, Sat-Sun 1100-1400; café Mon-Thu, Sun 0900-1400, Fri-Sat 0900-0400. Metro Banco de España. Map 4, C1/2/3, p253*

Calle Alcalá is a swaggering introduction to the Gran Vía, with which it connects on the eastern side of the city. It's lined with flamboyant belle époque buildings, like the glamorous Casino at number 15, (members only, unless you can talk the doormen into giving you a glimpse of the billowing staircase), and the beautiful art deco Círculo de Bellas Artes, now an excellent café-bar and cultural centre.

### Real Academia de Bellas Artes de San Fernando
C Alcalá 13. **T** 91 524 08 64. *Tue-Fri 0900-1900, Sat-Mon and holidays 0900-1430; guided visits Oct-Jun 1700 (Spanish only). €2.50/1.25 concessions. Free on Wed. Map 4, B9/10, p253*

The Royal Academy of Fine Arts has barely changed since Dalí was a student here in the 1920s, before he was expelled for questioning his professors' competence, and there's a lingering sense that the appreciation of art is a solemn business and any frivolity will be frowned upon. Nonetheless, the academy houses a surprisingly extensive collection of paintings and drawings (many of which were appropriated after the Jesuits were expelled from Spain in 1767) including works by El Greco, Velázquez, Zurbarán, Ribera, Murillo,

**!**
**●** The Calle Alcalá follows the route of an ancient pathway used for the *transhumancia*, the slow annual herding of sheep between the dusty south and the green north. The tradition was briefly revived a couple of years ago and the newspapers were full of surreal photographs of the Puerta de Alcalá knee-deep in an endless sea of sheep.

Titian, Rubens, Fragonard and Van Dyck. The academy is proudest of its large collection of paintings by Goya, including several of his later works which are imbued with an unsettling undercurrent.

## Torre Telefónica

Gran Vía 28. *Metro Gran Vía. Map 4, A8, p253*

Spain's first skyscraper, a slick, 29-storey art deco construction, was built in 1929 to house an American telephone company. As the most instantly recognisable landmark in the city centre, it was targeted by Franco's forces during the Civil War, and children used to collect the still-hot shrapnel embedded in its smooth façade. Spain's former national telephone company *Telefónica* owns the building and has invested billions in an exhibition space.

## Plaza de España

*Metro Plaza de España. Map 2, D2, p248*

The Plaza de España is a large, sandy square with a pair of huge ornamental fountains and a couple of grassy areas usually colonized by picnicking office-workers and the odd tramp. At the centre, Don Quixote and Sancho Panza sally forth, while Cervantes looks on gloomily. The square is overshadowed by two bombastic skyscapers: the Edificio de España (1948) and the Torre de Madrid (1957).

● *Sabatini Gardens (see p65) and the Templo de Debod (see p81) are a short stroll from the plaza, both are much prettier.*

## ★ Museo Cerralbo

C Ventura Rodríguez 17, **T** 91 547 36 46. *Tue-Sat 0930-1430, Sun 1000-1400. €2.50/1.25 concessions. Free on Sun and Wed. Map 2, D2, p248*

This beautiful 19th-century palace belonged to the 17th Marqués de Cerralbo, who crammed it with treasures picked up on his many travels. On his death in 1922 he bequeathed the palace and its contents to the state, with the stipulation that nothing was to be moved. As a result, it's delightfully, eccentrically cluttered, with Roman busts rubbing shoulders with Flemish tapestries, and paintings by Ribera, Murillo and Zurbarán jostle together in unfashionable proximity. The palace is fitted with breathtaking opulence; even the bathrooms are works of art, with pretty shell-shaped sinks and porcelain toilets. The chandelier collection is extraordinary; don't miss the ultra-kitsch pink-and-blue one in the Music Room.

## Plaza de Chueca

*Metro Chueca.  Map 5, H4, p254   See also p201*

Chueca is the heart of gay Madrid but it's also where most of the nightlife is concentrated. This square, with its terrace cafés and bars, may be quiet and nondescript by day, but it livens up dramatically at night and is a great place to start the night.

## Museo Municipal

C Fuencarral 78, **T** 91 588 86 72. *Tue-Fri 0930-2000, Sat-Sun 1000-1400. €1.80/0.90 concessions.  Metro Tribunal.  Map 5, F3, p254*

Madrid's town museum boasts one of the most extraordinary doorways in the city, a gushing Churrigueresque fantasy sculpted by Pedro de Ribera in the 17th century. Inside, there are plenty of plans and models, including Teixera's famous map made in 1656 (the first comprehensive map of Madrid), a huge wooden model of early 19th-century Madrid with a room to itself, and some delightful models of the mock-battles that used to take place on the Retiro lake (see p43). Upstairs there are more furnishings; a huge collection of porcelain from the long-demolished Real Fábrica de Buen Retiro; and a series of otherwise indifferent paintings that are fascinating for a glimpse into how Madrid used

### El Dos de Mayo

In early 1808 Napoleon's armies marched into Madrid with the cooperation of the cowardly Spanish king, Carlos IV. On 2 May, a carriage containing the royal family slipped out of the palace gates. Unfortunately, a local locksmith saw them and immediately assumed that the Napoleonic armies were spiriting them away. A crowd gathered yelling 'death to the French' and the city erupted into revolt. There are dozens of tales of heroic deeds, but none more so than the seamstress Mañuela Malasaña, after whom the neighbourhood is named, who was shot by the French soldiers after attacking them bravely with her scissors. Goya's celebrated works in the Prado, *El Dos de Mayo* (1808) and *El Tres de Mayo* (1808); see p33, were painted six years later to immortalize the heroism of the Madrileños against the French troops.

to look. Goya's famous *Allegory of Madrid* takes pride of place. When it was first painted in 1810, the frame held by the female figure contained a portrait of Napoleon, but when the French were being beaten back a few years later, the offending portrait was painted over. Then Napoleon returned to power and the painting had to be retouched again. The uncertain political climate meant the painting was eventually 'adjusted' seven times. Finally it was painted over with the words 2 de Mayo (Second of May), as a reminder of the uprising against the French occupiers (see box, p80).

### Plaza de Dos de Mayo
*Metro Malsaña. Map 5, E1, p254*

This square is named for the famous uprising against the French in 1808 (see box) and is the focal point of Malasaña's excellent nightlife, with plenty of terrace cafés, clubs and bars. It used to be the scene of a huge *botellón* every weekend, when a sea of teenagers would descend, clutching their plastic bottles of beer, wine and spirits (hence the name). But Madrid has cracked down firmly on the *botellón* and cleaners stand by with hoses to make sure they don't come back. Just off the square is Calle San Vicente Ferrer, which is sprinkled with old tiled shopfronts. At night this street is crammed pierced navel to pierced navel with hip students and teenagers queuing for the endless line of bars.

## Centro Cultural Conde Duque

Plaza Conde Duque 9-11, **T** 91 588 58 34. *Tue-Sat 1000-1400 and 1730-2100. Sat 1030-1330. Free. Metro Noviciado. Map 2, C2, p248*

This cultural centre puts on excellent temporary shows and is also the home of the city's large collection of contemporary art. Just to the north is the Plaza de los Comendadores, with a handful of hip terrace cafés, a good place for a post-museum drink.

## Parque del Oeste

Jardines de Templo del Debod, C Ferraz s/n, **T** 91 765 10 08. *Tue-Fri Apr-Sep 1000-1400 and 1800-2000, Oct-Mar 0945-1345, 1615-1815. Metro Ventura Rodríguez. Map 2, A1, p248*

This cool, shady park spreads along the western flank of the city just a few minutes' stroll north of the Plaza de España. One of its most surprising sights is a 2,000-year-old **Templo de Debod**, a gift from the Egyptians, perched on a low hill and reflected in a still pond in the south of the park. The surrounding peaceful gardens are very popular on Sunday mornings, when the benches are filled with locals reading their newspapers.

### Ermita de San Antonio de la Florida y Museo Panteón de Goya

Glorieta de la Florida 5, **T** 91 542 07 22. *Tue-Fri 1000-1400, 1600-2000, Sat-Sun 1000-1400. €1.80/0.90 concessions, free Wed and Sun. Metro Príncipe Pío. Head downhill along Calle Francisco y Jacinto Alcántara towards a pedestrian bridge which crosses the train tracks and leads to the Goya Pantheon.*

Goya was commissioned to decorate a new hermitage sheltering a cult statue of St Anthony of Padua in 1798. He worked rapidly, completing the frescoes in just 120 days and utterly transforming the simple chapel. In the cupola St Anthony raises a murdered man to life in order to exonerate his own father who had been unjustly accused of the crime. Around him swirl Goya's famous '*angelitas*', the plump, rosy-cheeked '*majas*' of La Latina and Lavapiés who appear in his joyful paintings of local festivals – except this time they have been transformed into angels. Goya's remains were brought here in 1919 and the chapel was closed for worship a decade later. The replica chapel directly opposite is used for services and is still the focus of a popular pilgrimage each year on 13 June.

### Teleférico and the Casa de Campo

Teleférico, Paseo Pintor Rosales s/n, **T** 91 541 74 50. *Mon-Fri 1200-2000, Sat-Sun and holidays 1100-2030. €2.80 single, €4 return. Metro Argüelles. Map 2, C1, p248 See Kids, p213*

Madrid's cable car sways giddily across the city and out to the vast Casa de Campo, a huge and beautiful park full of shady walks and cycling paths. There's a lake at the centre with cafés and a lively trade in prostitution which doesn't seem to faze anyone. There's a park information centre close to the lake which has information on botanic walks and wildlife. Also in the park are Madrid's zoo-aquarium and theme park, **Parque de Atracciones**.

★ **Highlights of Salamanca**

Best

- Museo Arqueológico, p92
- Museo Sorolla, p92
- Museo de Escultura al Aire Libre, p92
- Coffee and cakes at the Café Gijón, p153
- Shopping along Calle Serrano, p187

**Museo de América**

Av Reyes Católicos 6, **T** 91 549 2641. *Tue-Sat 1000-1500, Sun and holidays 1000-1430. €3/1.50 concessions. Free Sun. Metro Moncloa. Map2, A1, p248 See also Kids, p211*

This handsome, red-brick art deco museum displays Spain's collection of booty from the Americas and attempts to explain what Spain was doing there in the first place. It's large, extremely well laid out and there's plenty to amuse children, from shrunken heads and mummies, to slide shows and special family events. The highlights include 'The Treasure of the Quimbayas', the most important collection of pre-Columbian gold in the world, and an extremely rare Maya Codex (13th-16th centuries) that recounts the arrival of the Spanish.

● *Opposite is the Faro de Madrid, a glassy observation tower.*

# Salamanca, Paseo de Castellano and Ventas

*It's easy to feel overwhelmed in this part of the city; the 19th-century entrepreneurs built their broad avenues and flashy palaces here, and the 20th-century wheeler-dealers added a string of high-tech skyscrapers along the brutal **Paseo de Castellano** with its*

83

*constantly whizzing traffic.* **Salamanca** *has been a rich neighbourhood since the Marqués de Salamanca urged all his aristocratic
friends to buy into his new development on the northeastern fringe of
the city at the end of the 19th century. They came in droves, happy to
escape the insanitary medieval jumble of old Madrid for this elegant
grid of broad avenues and well-equipped mansions complete with
flush toilets. The neighbourhood is still Madrid's smartest district,
home to los yuppís, and their glossy offspring (pijos or pijas).
Salamanca is definitely the place to come if you want to exercise your
plastic; the streets (particularly Calles Serrano, Goya and Velázquez)
are lined with designer boutiques, swanky bars and chic restaurants.
The string of terrazas (bars and clubs with terraces) along the Paseo
de Castellano are still a fashionable spot to see and be seen, but if you
choose to party here, make sure you can hold your own against the
perfectly groomed locals.*

▸▸ *See Sleeping p127, Eating and drinking p151, Bars and clubs p167,
Shopping p187*

 ## Sights

---

### Palacio de Linares and Casa de América
Paseo Recoletos 2, **T** 91 595 48 00.  *Times and prices vary according
to the exhibitions. Metro Banco de España.  Map 3, B1, p250*

A century ago everyone who was anyone wanted a mansion along
the aristocratic Paseo de Recoletos. This is one of the few survivors,
an elegant palace set in handsome gardens which was built by the
Marqués de Linares in the 1890s. According to urban myth, the
palace is still haunted by the Marqués and his wife. The Marqués
defied his family and married a commoner, only to discover that
she was his half-sister. The unhappy couple were forced to divide
the palace into two apartments and live separately until their
deaths, and they still wail about their miserable fate on stormy

nights. The Palace has been sympathetically converted into the Casa de América, a cultural centre which hosts exhibitions, film events, lectures and concerts with a Latin American theme.

## Palacio Marqués de Salamanca
Paseo Recoletos 10.  *Not open to visitors.  Map 5, H8, p255*

The most flamboyant of the surviving palaces on the Paseo Recoletos, this was built for the Marqués de Salamanca, the entrepreneur behind the construction of the entire Salamanca district. An extravagant, larger-than-life character who made and lost three fortunes, he lived here with his remarkable art collection and Spain's first private bathroom until the loss of his final fortune forced him out to the suburbs where he died suddenly in 1883. Appropriately, it has been the headquarters of a Spanish bank since the early 20th century.

● *Opposite the palace is the legendary Café Gijón (see p153), one of the most famous literary cafés at the turn of the 20th century.*

## Centro Cultural de la Villa
Plaza de Colón s/n. **T** 91 575 60 80.  *Times and prices vary according to the exhibitions. Metro Colón.  Map 5, F9/G9, p255*

Madrid's subterranean cultural centre is built beneath the modern Plaza de Colón and hosts an impressive range of theatre, music and dance events (it is one of the main venues for the city's excellent dance festival, Madrid en Danza, see p181). The **Plaza de Colón** and the adjoining **Jardines de Descubrimiento** are dedicated to Christopher Columbus (Cristóbal Colón), with a monument to the explorer formed from vast blocks of sandstone surrounded by illuminated sheets of water.

## Biblioteca Nacional and Museo Interactivo del Libro

Paseo Recoletos 20, **T** 91 580 77 59.  *Tue-Sat 1000-2100, Sun 1000-1400. Free. Metro Serrano.  Map 5, G9, p255*

The largest and grandest building on the Paseo de Recoletos is the florid pompous National Library, built in the 19th century under Isabel II. It contains every book printed in Spain since 1712, plus manuscripts, drawings by Goya and Velázquez and the first book of Castillian (Spanish) grammar. Many of the library's treasures are too fragile to be handled, but the library has circumvented this problem and offers an engaging history of the library and its valuable collection in the adjoining Interactive Book Museum.

## Museo Arqueológico Nacional

C Serrano 13, **T** 91 577 79 12, www.man.es  *Tue-Sat 0930-2030, Sun 0930-1430. €3, free on Sat afternoon and Sun. Metro Serrano.  Map 5, G9, p255*

Madrid's enormous, gloomy archaeological museum is the most comprehensive in Spain, with a vast collection spanning several millennia. It shares the same building as the Biblioteca Nacional (see above) but the entrance is around the back on Calle Serrano. Although it's a tad old-fashioned and the labelling is exclusively in Spanish, there is plenty to keep your attention. Highlights include an excellent reproduction of the Altamira caves in Cantabria, discovered in 1879 but thought to have been painted around 8,5000 BC, in which bison, stags, and boars career across the walls with astonishing realism – one boar even scuttles by on several feet, obviously painted in order to create the illusion of rapid movement. The most important and most famous piece in the whole museum is the Dama de Elche, thought to have been sculpted around 500 BC, a mysterious bust of a woman whose enigmatic expression almost outdoes the Mona Lisa.

### ▶ Being Madridleño

Few Madrileños can boast four Madrileño grandparents. Like most capital cities, it's a big melting pot for people from all over the country as well as a liberal sprinkling of immigrants from further afield. But being Madrileño is still a matter of pride, wherever your family once came from. The *barrios bajos* are traditionally the most *castizo*, which literally means 'from Castile', but has come to mean authentically Madrileño. The inhabitants used to be known as *Manolos* (or *Manolas*), so called because the converted Jews who once lived here commonly named their eldest son Manolo. They were known for their sharp tongues and their sharp dress sense; the men rejected French fashions for the classic Spanish cape and hair net and the women famously tucked daggers in their stockings. Generations of travellers trawled the streets hoping for a glimpse of these romantic characters, but they had all but died out by the 19th century. Goya's Majos and Majas – similar in dress and attitude to the Manolos – live on in his cheerful depictions of 18th-century pilgrimages and festivals.

## Museo de Escultura al Aire Libre

Paseo de la Castellana (under the Paseo de Eduardo Dato). *Always open. Free. Metro Rubén Darío. Map 5, A10, p255*

Paseo de la Castellana is not a thing of beauty; streams of cars roar up it and it's lined with monstrous, glassy buildings. The Museum of Outdoor Sculpture comes as a particularly welcome oasis in this inhuman landscape, even if it is tucked underneath a flyover. There are about a dozen large works by some of Spain's best known sculptors, including Eduardo Chillida, Joan Miró and Julio González.

**Monumental Madrid**
*By day and by night Madrid's grandeur is there for all to see.*

## Urbanización AZCA and Torre Picasso

Paseo de la Castellana. *Beyond Museo Lázaro Galdiano  Metro Nuevos Ministerios.*

Just to the north of the grim, grey slabs of the Nuevos Ministerios (which house government buildings) is the Urbanización AZCA, a glittering, glassy complex of skyscrapers including Madrid's largest, the Torre Picasso which was designed by Minori Yamasaki, architect of New York's Twin Towers. Besides offices, it houses a huge shopping centre and dozens of bars and cafés.

## Plaza de Castilla and Las Torres Kio

*Metro Plaza de Castilla  Beyond Museo Lázaro Galdiano*

Madrid's most unusual contemporary buildings overlook the modern Plaza de Castilla; the towers are visible on the road between the centre and the airport. The twin towers of the Puerta de Europa (still better known as Las Torres KIO, after the Kuwait Investment Office, even though KIO were unable to raise the finance to complete them) lean in towards each other at an alarming angle, and were completed in 1996.

## Museo Lázaro Galdiano

C Serrano 122, **T** 91 561 60 84. *Closed for a major refurbishment in 2000 – expected to reopen late 2002 or early 2003; check with the tourist office. Metro Rubén Darío.  Map 2, A8, p249*

Don José Lázaro Galdiano amassed one of the most extraordinary private art collections in Madrid, which he bequeathed to the state on his death in 1942. It is displayed in the very elegant surroundings of his Italianate home in a quiet leafy corner of Salamanca. The collection is astonishingly eclectic and includes archaeological artefacts, paintings, sculptures, armour, furniture, jewellery and one of the finest collections of enamels and ivories in existence.

Among the paintings are works by Bosch, Rembrandt, Zurbarán, Velázquez, El Greco and Goya.

## Museo Sorolla

C General Martínez Camps 37, **T** 91 310 15 84. €2.40/1.20 concessions. Currently closed for restoration until late 2002; check with tourist office. Metro Rubén Darío. Map 2, A7, p249

This is one of Madrid's most delightful small museums, devoted to the Valenciano painter Joaquín Sorolla who lived here until his death in 1923. He enjoyed success both internationally and among Madrid's new bourgeoisie at the end of the 19th century. His luminous paintings borrowed some of the techniques of French Impressionism, but his figures and landscapes are modelled with a sharp clarity. The upper galleries display his light-filled, happy paintings of children and pretty country scenes. The lower floor has been left intact to give some insight into the artist's everyday life. Light streams in from the huge skylights in his studio and the living areas display jewellery, religious medals and other bits collected on his travels. The house stands in a tiny Moorish-style garden, deliciously cool in summer, with palms, tiles and fountains.

## La Residencia de Estudiantes

C Pinar 23, **T** 91 563 64 11. Times and prices vary. Usually closed Sat afternoon and Sun. Metro Gregorio Marañón. Above Museo Soralla

The Students' Residence (usually known simply as el resi) was completed in 1915 and rapidly became one of the most influential and dynamic institutions in Spain. Famously, it was here that Lorca, Dalí and Buñuel met and became friends in the 1920s, developing their ground-breaking theories about art and literature. After the Civil War, el resi stultified under Franco's repressive regime, but it is now undergoing a dramatic refurbishment and hosts some of the most stimulating temporary exhibitions in Madrid.

### Fundación Juan March

C/Castelló 77, T91 435 42 40. *Mon-Sat 1000-1400, 1730-2100, Sun and hols 1000-1400. Free.   Map 2, B9, p249*

This cultural centre was established by the Catalan tycoon Juan March in the 1950s (before he got banged up for cooking the books in the 1970s). It hosts excellent temporary exhibitions and major retrospectives and offers a regular programme of music concerts.

### Plaza de Toros Monumental de las Ventas

C Alcalá 237, Plaza de las Ventas, **T** 91 725 18 57. *Tue-Fri 0930-1430. Sun 1000-1300. Free. Metro Ventas.   Map 2, B12, p249*

There's nothing to see in the mainly residential neighbourhood of Ventas except Madrid's bullring. The 'Cathedral of Bullfighting' as it is often called is the largest bullring in Spain, built in the 1930s, with capacity for 22,300 spectators. The **bullfighting museum** is at the back, near the horses' stables, with portraits of famous bullfighters, costumes, *banderillas* (the plumed daggers used to slow down the bull) and the stuffed heads of famous bulls. Most gruesome of all are the bloodstained clothes which belonged to some of the *toreros* who met their deaths in the bullring; one of the most recent was Yiyo, who died here in 1985 and is commemorated by a statue outside the ring.

**Museums and galleries**

**Listings**

## Museums and galleries

- **Museo Lázaro Galdiano** An eclectic collection containing a world-class enamel and ivory display, p92.
- **Museo Municipal** Models and paintings show how Madrid has evolved over the centuries, p79.
- **Museo Nacional de Artes Decorativas** Antique furnishings, including a large display of doll's houses, p42.
- **Museo Nacional Centro de Arte Reina Sofía** 20th-century art, including Picasso's *Guernica*, housed in a beautifully converted hospital, p37.
- **Museo Naval** Maritime history focussing on 15th and 16th-century exploration, p43.
- **Museo Sorolla** Artist Joaquín Sorolla's house, delightfully preserved, p92.
- **Museo Taurino** Gory museum of bullfighting, p92.
- **Museo Thyssen-Bornemisza** Pieces from the Italian Primitives to Pollock are on show in this wide-ranging collection, p39.
- **Palacio de Linares and Casa de América** Latin American events in a palace haunted by an incestuous Marqués, p84.
- **Palacio de Veláquez and Palacio de Cristal** These two 19th-century pavilions provide an elegant backdrop for temporary modern-art exhibitions, p44.
- **Palacio Real** A monument to Royal opulence, p62.
- **Observatorio Astronómico Nacional** A charming observatory overlooking the pretty Retiro, p44.
- **Real Academia de Bellas Artes de San Fernando** The art academy where Dalí studied… and was expelled. Contains a large collection by Goya, p77.
- **Real Fábrica de Tapices** Tapestry workshops that still use 18th-century techniques, p45.

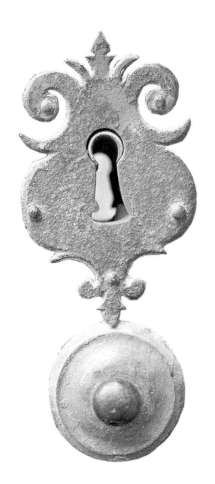

**San Lorenzo de El Escorial and Valle de los Caídos 97** Immense palace–monastery, burial place of kings, and Franco's outsized tomb and monument to the fallen, in craggy mountains with beautiful views.

**Segovia 99** A golden city known for its storybook castle , incredibly tall Roman aqueduct and roast suckling pig. Go during the week to avoid the crowds.

**Toledo 102** Ancient cultured city on a hilltop, once a centre of religious tolerance , with a great collection of works by El Greco.

**Avila 107** Contemplative mountain town inside magnificent medieval walls, birthplace of visionary Santa Teresa.

**Aranjuez 110** A blissful retreat from the heat in spectacular gardens famed throughout Spain and another guilded palace.

**Alcalá de Henares 111** An affluent city from Spain's Golden age, birthplace of Cervantes and home to a famous university, overhanging houses and excellent shops.

# San Lorenzo de El Escorial and Valle de los Caídos

*On a clear day, you can see a huge, pale cross emerging from the backdrop of the mountains north of Madrid. This is the **Valle de los Caídos**, Franco's enormous monument to the fallen of the Civil War, which became his tomb and is still a surprisingly popular day trip for los nostálgicos, the name for those who whisper that things were better in the old days. Close by is the little town of **San Lorenzo de El Escorial** where another megalomaniac ruler, Felipe II, ordered the construction of the vast palace-monastery of El Escorial, burial place of a dozen Spanish monarchs. The town is rather more cheerful than the palace which has brought it fame, and it's a favourite weekend destination for Madrileños who come to enjoy the restaurants and the cool mountain air. It's also a good base for walkers who want to explore the beautiful mountains of the **Sierra de Guadarrama**.*
▸▸ *See Eating and drinking p154*

*Regular buses (every 20 mins, less at weekends) with Herranz from Moncloa bus station to the central bus station in San Lorenzo. One bus daily leaves from El Escorial for Valle de los Caídos at 1515, returns at 1730. Regular trains from Atocha to San Lorenzo de El Escorial take 1 hour. It is then a delightful 2-km walk from the station to the monastery, or you can take the local shuttle bus.*

## Palacio Real de San Lorenzo de El Escorial
**T** 91 890 59 02/3/4, www.patrimonionacional.es  *Apr-Sep Tue-Sun 1000-1800, Oct-Nov Tue-Sun 1000-1700. €5.95, €6.90 including guided visit/concessions €5. Audioguide in English €1.80. Cloakroom €1. Café and shop.*

Felipe II's vast palace-monastery looms above the mountain town of El Escorial, 42 km northwest of Madrid. The king threw himself into his pet project with such fanatical devotion that poor Madrid, his brand new capital, was completely ignored. Building began under Juan Bautista de Toledo in 1563 and was continued by Juan de Herrera. The last stone of the massive complex – monastery, palace, pantheon and library – was finally laid under the king's watchful gaze in 1584. Few admit to liking it but no one can fail to be impressed by the staggering proportions.

The tour begins at the **Bourbon apartments**. El Escorial was far too depressing for the frivolous Bourbons, who spent little time here, but their apartments contain some beautiful tapestries by Goya. Beneath these rooms, two museums are housed in the cellars: the **Museo de Pintura**, with works by Veronese, Titian, Van Dyck, Rubens, van der Weyden and Ribera among others; and the **Museo de Arquitectura**, which shows the original plans for the monastery along with some of the equipment used for hauling the huge hunks of granite.

The **Habsburg apartments** are unexpectedly intimate, prettily decorated with blue-and-white tiles. You can see the specially designed chair in which gout-ridden Felipe II was carried by his long-suffering servants, who had to put up with the stench of their master's gouty leg as well as his manic eccentricities, and the bed in which he died in 1598, carefully placed so that he could hear mass from the basilica directly below.

When Felipe died, he was buried in the **Panteón de los Reyes** (Royal Pantheon), where a dozen Spanish monarchs are buried in a flurry of gold and marble. Next to the pantheon is the Rotting Room (sealed off, thankfully), where the bodies of dead monarchs are left to rot and dry out before being placed in the pantheon.

The **Salas Capitulares** (Chapter Halls) contain more of El Escorial's enormous art collection, gathered underneath elaborately painted 16th-century ceilings. The Basilica is the very heart of the complex, repressively dark, cold and gloomy. It contains 43 altars so that several masses could be held simultaneously; just two chapels, at the back, were for commoners.

### Casita del Príncipe and Casita del Infante

*Casita del Príncipe has guided tours Apr-Sep Sat, Sun and public holidays 1000-1300 and 1600-1830. Must be booked in advance on T 91 890 59 02/03. €3.45. Casita del Infante is open Holy Week and Jul-Sep Tue-Sun 1000-1845. €3.*

These are two small palaces downhill towards El Escorial town, both pretty Bourbon extravagances: the Casita del Príncipe, surrounded by lush gardens, and the delightfully frivolous Casita del Infante.

### Valle de los Caídos

*Apr-Sep Tue-Sun 0930-1900, Oct-Mar daily 1000-1800. €5, free on Wed to EU passport holders.*

Franco's tomb and monument to the fallen (or *caídos*) of the Civil War was begun in 1940, using Republican prisoners as labourers. The setting, a craggy mountain valley with endless views, is beautiful, but the monument itself is pompous, overblown and brutally ugly. The vast basilica is built into the rock and topped with an outsized cross (supposedly the largest in the world). Franco is buried by the altar, and the monument has become a focal point for the bizarre rally held on the anniversary of his death, on 20 November.

# Segovia

*Segovia is one of the most captivating cities in central Spain, built of golden stone, capped with a fairy tale castle and set against the dramatic peaks of the Sierra de Guadarrama. It's almost as famous for its sturdy Castillian cuisine – with its legendary speciality of* **cochinillo** *(roast suckling pig), traditionally slaughtered at just 21 days old – as it is for the enormous* **Roman aqueduct** *which has stood here for two millennia. It's the perfect place to relax (although not at weekends when everyone else is doing it too). If you decide to* *spend more than a day here there are gentle walks along the **Eresma river** or tougher treks among the surrounding peaks.*

▸▸ *See Eating and drinking p154*

---

*Regular buses leave from Paseo de la Florida 11 (Metro Príncipe Pío) every 30 mins with La Sepulvadena taking 1 hour 15 mins. Trains leave every 2 hours from Atocha and take 2 hours. Segovia station is 2 km from the town centre; take bus no 3 from outside the station.*

## Roman aqueduct

Nothing holds together the 25,000 stones of this soaring two-storey aqueduct which stretches for 760 m and arches a giddy 29 m above Plaza Azoguejo. The tallest surviving Roman aqueduct, it was still carrying water to the city right up until a generation or two ago, but pollution and traffic vibration have taken their toll in recent years.

---

## Catedral

Plaza Mayor. *Mar-Oct 1000-1830, Nov-Feb 1000-1730. €2/1.20. Museum closed Sun mornings.*

Rising serenely above the Plaza Mayor, Segovia's cathedral was built between 1525 and 1590 in what is probably the latest example of the Gothic style in Spain. Inside there is some elegant vaulting in the chapels surrounding the ambulatory, but little else to see. Just off the delicate cloister is the Sala Capitular, where the cathedral's scant treasures are gathered.

---

## Alcázar

Plaza de la Reina Victoria Eugenia, **T** 921 46 07 59. *Apr-Sep 1000-1900; Oct Mon-Fri 1000-1800, Sat-Sun 1000-1900; Nov-Mar 1000-1800. €3/2.25. Free on Tue for EU passport holders. Audioguide €3.*

Segovia's Alcázar sits on a cliff edge, bristling with storybook turrets and spires. Purists sniff that the current version, a fanciful

19th-century restoration, bears no resemblance to the original, but Disney apparently liked it so much they used it as a model for their first theme park. The interior has been fitted out with armour and weapons, but the real highlights are the spectacular *artesonado* ceilings that glitter magnificently in almost every room. There's a 144-step hike up the old watchtower for stupendous views out across the rooftops to the mountains, still snowcapped in late spring.

### Iglesia de la Vera Cruz
*Apr-Sep daily 1030-1300 and 1530-1900, Oct-Mar Tue-Sun 1030-1300 and 1530-1800. €1.50.*

The little 13th-century Iglesia de la Vera Cruz, also built with Segovia's warm, honey-coloured stone, sits just outside the city walls. Its fortunes have declined in the past few centuries and even the sliver of the True Cross which gave it its name has gone to another local church.

### Palacio Real de La Granja de San Ildefonso and Palacio Real de Riofrío
*www.patrimonionacional.es   Both palaces open 26 Mar-7 Oct Tue-Sun 1000-1800, 8 Oct-25 Mar Tue-Fri 1000-1330, 1500-1700, Sat-Sun 1000-1400. Visits by guided tour only (in several languages). €4.81 (to both)/€3.91 concessions. Free on Wed to EU passport holders. La Granja is a 10-min bus ride away, but you'll need your own transport to get to Riofrío, 12 km from La Granja.*

These are two sumptuous royal palaces close to Segovia. **La Granja**, a frothy Italian-style palace built for the Bourbon monarchs, is surrounded by magnificent gardens, famous for their fountains and sculptures. Unfortunately, you can only see the fountains in all their glory on two days a year, normally 25 July and 25 August (they turn on a few on Wednesdays and weekends to whet your appetite). Entry to the adjoining **Museo de Tapices**

(Tapestry Musuem) and the **Colegiata** are both included in the ticket price. If you've been dazzled by the palace's gorgeous crystal chandeliers, you can find out how they were made at the former **Real Fábrica de Cristales** (Royal Crystal Factory).

The palace at **Riofrío** is hidden away in beautiful woodland and attracts fewer visitors than La Granja, which can be a charm in itself. Despite its grand scale, Riofrío was merely a hunting lodge and now half of it has been given up to a bizarre museum of hunting, completely with row upon row of stuffed heads.

# Toledo

*Toledo is an enchanting city of narrow, winding streets, sitting on a hilltop beside the **River Tajo**. It's been an important settlement since long before the Romans conquered it in the second century BC, and succeeding waves of conquerors and settlers have all left their mark here. During the Middle Ages, it gained a formidable reputation for learning and religious tolerance, and Muslims, Jews and Christians lived together in comparative harmony. Cultured, prosperous Toledo was in the running for capital, but when Madrid won the race in 1561, it lost most of its influence and became a quiet backwater. **El Greco** retired here after refusing to butter up his royal patrons in Madrid, and the city holds an extensive collection of his works, some of which can be seen in the **Casa-Museo de El Greco**. Toledo has done a good job of packaging its past for the tourists who arrive by the bus-load during summer. Come in low season or stay overnight if you can; when the day-trippers are gone and quiet falls on the ancient town, it remains one of the most beguiling cities in Spain.*

▸▸ *See Eating and drinking p155*

*Buses every hour taking 1½ hours with Galiano Contintental from Estación Sur de Autobuses (Metro Méndez Alvaro). It's a 15-minute uphill walk to the city gates. Trains take 1 hour and depart every 90 mins from Atocha station. From the station it is a 20-minute walk.*

## Catedral

C Cardenal Cisneros s/n, **T** 92 522 22 41.  *Mon-Sat, Sun 1400-1800. €4.80 (includes entrance to all sections).*

Toledo's enormous cathedral was built on the ruins of a great mosque. The vast interior is surprisingly light and contains a remarkable Gothic Choir carved with scenes from the conquest of Granada and a rich menagerie of fabulous creatures. Behind the main altar is the enormous, fluffy baroque transparente, with saints and angels oozing out of the roof on clouds of plaster. The Treasury has a spectacular *artesonado* ceiling which looks like a melting honeycomb and a 10-foot-high 16th-century silver monstrance. In the sacristy are the cathedral's paintings, including El Greco's magnificent *El Expolio* (Disrobing of Christ), and works by Rubens, Zurbarán, Titian, Raphael and Caravaggio.

## Museo de Santa Cruz

C Cervantes 3, **T** 92 522 10 36. *Mon 1000-1400, 1600-1830, Tue-Sat 1000-1830, Sun 1000-1430. Free.*

The former hospital of Santa Cruz has been handsomely refurbished to hold the city's art collection and is set around a wide, light-filled cloister. The basement contains prehistoric artefacts, including the skull and tusks of a couple of mammoths. The painting and sculpture galleries are housed on the ground floor and include a mixed collection of 16th- and 17th-century religious art, a whole gallery of El Grecos and the magnificent *Tapis de los Astrolabios* (Signs of the Zodiac), a 15th-century Flemish tapestry.

**Bishops behind bars**
The sculpture-encrusted Gothic cathedral at Toledo dominates this fortress town, one-time capital of Spain.

## Alcázar
Cuesta de Carlos V, **T** 92 522 16 73. *Tue-Sun 0930-1400. €2.*

Toledo's Alcázar (fortress) sits right on the top of the hill but most of what you see today is a reconstruction, as it was almost entirely demolished during the Civil War. In 1936, almost 1,200 Nationalists holed up here for 68 days while Republican forces bombarded the fortress. This is one of the few places where Franco still gets a good press, with plenty of patriotic plaques and photos of medal ceremonies for siege-survivors. Most bizarrely, the Nationalist commander's office has been left as it was at the end of the siege to provide a setting for a taped 'genuine' telephone conversation between the commander and his son, who was being held by the Republicans. The Colonel tells his son: "Commend your soul to God, shout *Viva España*, and die like a patriot". The rest of the fortress is an army museum, with an enormous collection of weaponry, models, medals and uniforms.

## Casa-Museo de El Greco
C Samuel Leví s/n, **T** 925 22 40 46. *Tue-Sat 1000-1345, 1600-1745, Sun 1000-1345. €3/1.50 concessions. The house is currently under restoration but you can visit the museum for a reduced price.*

It seems unlikely that El Greco ever actually lived here, but it remains a beautiful example of a 16th-century Toledo mansion, with a recreation of El Greco's studio on the upper floor. A small museum displays several of El Greco's masterpieces, including a magnificent *View of Toledo* (1610-16) in a small chapel with a richly gilded *artesonado* ceiling. Fans of El Greco's work shouldn't miss the **Iglesia de Santo Tomé**, where his painting of the *Burial of the Count of Orgaz* is displayed above the Count's tomb.

### Sinagoga del Tránsito/Museo Sefardí

C Samuel Levi s/n, **T** 92 522 36 65. *Tue-Sat 1000-1400, 1600-1800, Sun 1000-1400. Currently closed for restoration. €2.40.*

Before the Jews were expelled from Spain in 1492, Toledo had the largest Jewish community on the Iberian peninsula. This is one of just two synagogues which have survived – once there were 10 – and it was promptly converted into a church in 1492. The Mozarabic interior has been decorated with intricate tilework and there's a dazzling *artesonado* ceiling. The annexe, once a convent, has been converted to house a fascinating museum of Sephardic Jewish culture, with tombs, columns, clothing and books.

# Avila

*The austere mountain town of Avila is set on a windswept plateau, surrounded by the chilly granite peaks of the **Sierra de Gredos**. The reddish-brown tangle of medieval mansions and Romanesque churches is completely enclosed by magnificent medieval walls, studded with towers and crenellations. This 'city of saints and stones' is also the birthplace of **Santa Teresa**, the 16th-century mystic, visionary and writer, and is still a major pilgrimage centre. It remains a hushed and contemplative city, but if it all gets too much, escape to the surrounding mountains which are a haven for hikers and climbers. While you are here, try some yemas, a delicious sticky sweet made of egg yolk and sugar, traditionally made by Avila's nuns.*

▶▶ See Eating and drinking, p155

*Buses take1 hour 45 minutes and leave every 2 hours from Estación Sur with Larrear. Frequent trains (1 hour 30 minutes) go across the mountains from Chamartín and Atocha stations.*

### Muralla de Avila

Entrance at the Puerta de Catedral, **T** 92 010 21 21. *Tue-Sun 1100-2000 (last entrance at 1915). Guided visits in Spanish only at 1115, 1215, 1315, 1715, 1815, 1915. €3.50/2 concessions.*

Constructed in the wake of Alfonso VI's victory in Toledo, these massive walls were erected to ensure that the Muslim forces could not reconquer the city. Twelve metres high, 3 m thick, and studded with nine gates and 88 towers, they became legendary even as they were being built. A short section has been made into a panoramic walkway, with views out over the old city, and up to the peaks of the Sierra de Gredos.

● *For the best views of the walls themselves, head to the little shrine at Cuatro Postes just outside town on the Salamanca road.*

### Catedral

Plaza de Catedral, **T** 92 021 16 41. *Apr-May, Mon-Fri 1000-1900, Sat 1000-1900, Sun and holidays 1200-1900; Jun-Oct Mon-Sat 1000-2000, Sun and holidays 1200-2000; Nov-Mar Mon-Fri 1030-1330 and 1530-1730, Sat 1000-1730. €2.50.*

As the massive city walls were being erected to defend the city from the Moors, the cathedral was engaged in the struggle for souls. It was incorporated into the walls to become a literal and metaphorical bastion and the austere façade betrays its dual function as a fortress and place of worship. The interior is surprisingly lovely, with its lofty Gothic nave made of rosy stone and magnificent Plateresque stalls and retrochoir. The cloister, attractively rumpled and overgrown, is home to several storks' nests; just off it is the cathedral museum, with a disappointing collection of paintings and religious ornaments.

## Monasterio Real de Santo Tomás

Plaza de Granada 1, **T** 92 022 04 00. *1000-1300, 1600-2000. Free; €1 for cloisters. From Plaza de Santa Teresa it's a 15-min walk downhill.*

This Dominican monastery is set around three cloisters and was established at the end of the 15th century by the Catholic Kings. It did service as their summer residence, and was also the seat of Avila's university. But its glory days have long gone, and grass sprouts through the cracks in the paving stones. The second cloister, the Cloister of Silence, is handsomely decorated with engravings on the upper gallery and a small staircase leads up to an exquisitely carved Gothic choir which gives a beautiful birds'-eye-view of the elegant Gothic church. The sumptuous alabaster tomb behind the main altar belongs to Don Juan, the only son of the Catholic Kings, whose premature death opened the door to the Habsburg dynasty.

## Museo de Santa Teresa

C La Dama. **T** 92 021 10 30. *Apr-Oct 1000-1400 and 1600-1900; Nov-Mar 1000-1330 and 1530-1730. €2.*

The Convento de Santa Teresa, also known as the Convento de la Santa, was built on the site where Teresa of Avila was born. A new museum devoted to the life of the saint has been established around the corner on Calle La Dama. The setting, a stone cellar, is attractive, but the exhibits are extremely dull. The most interesting section is at the end, where photographs of more recent Carmelite saints are displayed, including one of Edith Stein (Santa Teresa Benedicta de la Cruz) who died at Auschwitz.

# Aranjuez

*Lush Aranjuez is a rare oasis of green in the sun-baked Castillian plain. There's another extravagant **Bourbon palace**, a favourite **Royal retreat** in summer, but Aranjuez is most famous for the exquisite **gardens** which stretch for miles and miles, as well as a fascinating **Royal barge museum**. The local specialities are strawberries and asparagus; if you arrive on the Tren de la Fresa 'Strawberry Train' (see below), they'll serve you plump local strawberries on the way.*

▸▸ *See Eating and drinking p156*

---

*Buses take an hour and leave every 30 mins with* Autominibus Urbanos *from Estación Sur de Autobuses (Metro Méndez Alvaro). Trains take 45 mins and leave every 10 mins from Atocha station. Local buses leave from the station into town; to walk, turn right out of the station and left on the main road. Tren de la Fresa goes to Aranjuez from Atocha station on summer weekends late Apr until mid-Oct.*

---

### Palacio de Aranjuez

*T 91 891 13 44. Oct-Mar 1000-1715, Apr-Sep 1000-1815. €4.81/3.91. Free to EU passport holders on Wed.*

Indolent royals looking for a retreat from the burning heat of Madrid built themselves an impressive palace in the late 16th century and surrounded it with spectacular gardens which are still justly famed throughout Spain (see below). The palace will hold no surprises for anyone who has seen the Palacio Real in Madrid, or the other royal palaces in San Lorenzo or Riofrío (see p97 and 101), but it's still worth a visit. The guided tour runs through one gilded salon after another, all dripping with gold flounces and crystal chandeliers. The most over-the-top room bulging with ornamentation is Isabel II's dazzling golden bedroom.

### Jardines de la Isla and the Parterre and Jardines del Príncipe

Jardines de la Isla and Parterre are behind the Palacio de Aranjuez; the entrance to the Jardines del Príncipe is on C de la Reina.
*Oct-Mar 0800-1830, Apr-Sep 0800-2030. Free.*

The main attraction of Aranjuez is undoubtedly its remarkable gardens. Behind the palace is the formal, manicured expanse of the Jardines de la Isla and the Parterre, which combine elements of Italian, French, Dutch and Islamic garden design. The most extensive gardens are the cool and shady Jardines del Príncipe, which stretch along the riverbank (cross the Parterre and go over the roundabout to find them). These beautiful gardens are filled with trees, walkways, ponds and perfumed rose gardens where you can escape the heat in summer for several blissful hours. At the furthest end of the gardens is the delightful little **Casa del Labrador**, T 91 891 03 05, a pretty pink mini-palace. Close to the river is the **Museo de Faluas Reales** (Royal barge museum), T 91 891 24 53, where you can gawp at the gilded ship used to transport languid Royals downriver. You can only visit the palace and museum on a guided tour. Book well in advance.

# Alacalá de Henares

*Alcalá de Henares claim to fame was its University, which was established by Cardinal Cisneros (confessor to Isabel II) in 1498, and which came to rival even that of Salamanca as the intellectual centre of Spain. **Cervantes** was born here and Calderón de la Barca, Lope de Vega and Ignacio Loyola all studied here during Spain's Golden Age. The University was moved to Madrid in the 19th century and the city went into decline, which has been dramatically reversed since the University's return to Alcalá some years ago. Now it's an engaging, quietly affluent city scattered with plenty of opulent reminders of the glory days of the 16th and 17th centuries, like the **Colegio de San***

*Ildefonso. The charming main street, with its medieval arcades, excellent shops and overhanging houses leads to the delightful little **Casa-Museo de Cervantes**.*

▸▸ *See Eating and drinking p156*

---

*Frequent buses take 50 mins with* Continental Auto *from Av de América 34, Metro Cartagena. Frequent trains take 40 mins from Atocha and Chamartín. Tren de Cervantes runs from Atocha to Alcalá de Henares on weekends from mid-Apr to mid-Jun, and late Sep until early Dec. Departs 1100 and returns at 1900.*

---

## Colegio de San Ildefonso

Plaza de San Diego, **T** 91 885 40 00. *Guided visits only (hourly 1130-1330 and 1700-1900, more frequently at weekends).* €2.10.

The pale, splendid Colegio de San Ildefonso has an elaborate, graceful Plateresque façade and a magnificent great hall (*Paraninfo*) with a sumptuous, densely carved Mudéjar ceiling, where the ceremony for Spain's most influential literary award, the Prix Cervantes, is held annually on 23 April. The University's founder Cardinal Cisneros is buried in the beautiful chapel of San Ildefonso, which has another wonderful Renaissance *artesonado* ceiling and elaborately stuccoed walls.

---

## Casa-Museo de Cervantes

Corner of C Mayor and C Imagen, **T** 91 889 96 54. *Tue-Sun 1015-1330 and 1600-1815. Free.*

This is a reproduction of the house where Cervantes was born in 1547. His father was a bloodletter who worked in the neighbouring hospital (which is Spain's oldest and still going strong). The rooms are arranged around a pretty, tiled patio with a quiet fountain and are filled with period furniture and rare old editions of *Don Quixote*.

Strangely, Madrid has few hotels which are truly charming. At the top end, there are some beautiful, luxurious palaces which have become the favoured retreats of film stars and celebrities, but there are many more bland international chain hotels offering excellent amenities but little in the way of character. Most budget hotel rooms are uniform browns with nylon bedding and battered furniture, but the Spanish are fanatic housekeepers and they are usually spotless. There are a few enterprising places with bright, modern decor and internet access. You will be usually be offered an interior or an exterior room – exterior rooms have balconies but are noisy and interior rooms are often dark. Balcony or not, bring some industrial strength ear plugs; Madrid is a very noisy city.

Finding accommodation in Madrid is no longer as easy as it once was; book as far in advance as possible. The Brújula booking agency, Calle Princesa 1, T 91 559 9705, takes advance bookings for Madrid and surrounding towns. They charge a fee of about €2.

| € | Sleeping codes | | | |
|---|---|---|---|---|
| **AL** | €250 and over | **D** | €60-90 |
| **A** | €180-250 | **E** | €40-60 |
| **B** | €130-180 | **F** | €20-40 |
| **C** | €90-130 | **G** | €20 and under |

Prices are for a double room in high season

In general, most moderate to inexpensive accommodation is clustered in nightlife areas around the Plaza Santa Ana or north of the Gran Vía in Chueca and Malasaña. Smart Salamanca has the upmarket business hotels and a few chi-chi boutique hotels, while around the Plaza Mayor and the Palacio Real are traditional hotels in the moderate to expensive price range. La Latina and Lavapiés have little in the way of accommodation as yet, but now that gentrification has well and truly set in it can only be a matter of time.

# Paseo del Prado and around

### Hotels

**AL Ritz**, Plaza de la Lealtad 5, **T** 91 701 6767, **F** 91 701 6776, www.ritz.es *Metro Banco de España. Map 3, D1, p250* Madrid's *Grande Dame* of the hotel world, this lavish, creamy confection has a wonderful setting right by the Prado. Pure luxury, with a fine restaurant and chic cocktail bar which was a favourite with Dalí. The leafy terrace with thickly cushioned wicker chairs is a delight in summer.

**B Nacional**, Paseo del Prado 48, **T** 91 429 66 29, **F** 91 369 1564, www.hotelnhnacional.com *Metro Banco de España. Map 3, G1, p250* This elegant mansion built around 1900 is now part of the

Sleeping

115

NH chain, and sits right in the middle of the three art museums. Rooms are spacious and well-equipped if not exactly oozing with charm.

**C  Mediodía**, Plaza del Emperador Carlos V 8, **T** 91 527 30 60. *Metro Atocha. Map 3, H1, p250* Classic 19th-century hotel near Atocha station. It may a bit down on its luck nowadays with bus tours providing much of its business, but the rooms are spacious and there's still a faint whiff of the old glamour.

**E  Mora**, Paseo del Prado 32, **T** 91 420 05 64, **F** 91 429 15 69. *Metro Banco de España. Map 4, F12, p253* Simple hotel which is much sought-after for its perfect location just opposite the Botanic Gardens and the Prado. Rooms were renovated a few years ago and are clean and bright.

### Hostales

**F  Hostal Residencia La Coruña**, Paseo del Prado 12, **T** 91 429 25 43. *Metro Atocha. Map 4, E12, p253* Tiny, friendly little *pensión* within a stone's throw of the Prado. Six spotless rooms sharing two bathrooms. Closed August.

# Sol, Huertas and Santa Ana

### Hotels

**AL  Palace**, Plaza de las Cortes 7, **T** 91 360 80 00, **F** 91 360 81 00, www.palacemadrid.com *Metro Sevilla. Map 4, D11, p253* Dripping with chandeliers and crawling with liveried footman, this sumptuous belle époque-style hotel offers luxury on a grand scale. It's perfectly located for the three big museums of the Paseo del Arte.

**AL  Villa Real**, Plaza de las Cortes 10, **T** 91 420 37 67, **F** 91 420 02 47, www.derbyhotels.es  *Metro Sevilla*.  *Map 4, D10, p253*  Chic boutique-style hotel, with large, ochre-painted rooms decorated with a stylish mix of antiques and modern art and sculpture. Two fine restaurants (one, *East 47*, does excellent gourmet tapas), sauna and gym. Suites are available with jacuzzis for a real splurge.

**B  Palacios**, C Preciados 37, **T** 91 454 44 00, **F** 91 454 44 01. *Metro Sol*.  *Map 4, B6, p252*  Brand-new four-star hotel on one of the city centre's main shopping streets; pristine modern rooms set in a former 19th-century palace which has retained its old staircase and fittings.

**B  Tryp Reina Victoria**, Plaza de Santa Ana 14, **T** 91 531 45 00, **F** 91 522 03 07. *Metro Sol*.  *Map 4, F10, p253*  A famous belle époque-style hotel which looks like it should be by the seaside somewhere. Historically, bullfighters have always stayed here and there is a plaque to Manolete (see p50) at the entrance.

**C  Asturias**, C Sevilla 2, **T** 91 429 66 76, **F** 91 429 40 36, www.chh.es  *Metro Sevilla*.  *Map 4, C9, p253*  This handsome, old hotel is close to the Puerta del Sol; inside rooms are the quietest, but the outside rooms have wrought-iron balconies for watching the action on the street below.

**D  Moderno**, C Arenal 2, **T** 91 531 09 00, **F** 91 531 35 50, info@hotel-moderno.com  *Metro Sol*.  *Map 4, C6, p252*  Agreeable, modest hotel which has been recently renovated and offers good value for the amenities.

**D  Paris**, C Alcalá 2, **T** 91 521 64 91, **F** 91 531 01 88. *Metro Sol*.  *Map 4, C8, p253*  One of the most historic hotels in the city, this was once the luxury choice par excellence. A century (and a couple of refurbishments) later, the rooms have become a monument to 1960s kitsch. Still, it does offer a creaky, old-fashioned charm and the Tío Pepe sign still blazes from the rooftop.

## Hostales

**D Hospedaje Madrid**, C Esparteros 6, **T** 91 522 00 60, **F** 91 532 35 10, www.hospedajemadrid.com *Metro Sol. Map 6, A6, p256* Friendly, welcoming hostal which has been completely overhauled and offers modern, attractive rooms decorated with pine or wrought iron furniture. En suite bathrooms with hairdryers, a/c, and TV are among the facilities. They also have five attractive apartments, with washing machines and bright, modern furnishings. Doubles from e66 and apartments from €84 per night.

**D Hostal Persal**, Plaza del Angel 12, **T** 91 369 46 43, **F** 91 369 19 52, hostal.persal@mad.servicom.es *Metro Sol. Map 4, E8, p253* Smart, attractively furnished *hostal*, with spacious rooms and very helpful staff. One of the most popular choices in the city – and consequently almost always full.

**E Hostal Adriano**, C Cruz 26, **T/F** 91 209 02 07, www.hostaladriano.com *Metro Sol. Map 4, D8, p253* Newly opened *hostal* which offers fantastic amenities for budget travellers; free internet access from all rooms (with your own laptop), as well as telephones and fridges. Bright rooms with cheerful painted walls and modern furnishings. Highly recommended.

**E Hostal Astoria**, C Carrera de San Jerónimo 30-32, **T** 91 429 11 88, **F** 91 429 20 23, info@hostal-astoria.com *Metro Sol. Map 4, D9, p253* High up on the fifth floor of a lovely 19th-century building, this is a very comfortable *hostal* with attractive rooms decorated in light floral prints, en suite bathrooms with hairdryers and efficient staff.

E **Hostal Barrera**, C Atocha 96, **T** 91 527 53 81, **F** 91 527 39 50, www.hostalbarrera.com *Metro Atocha. Map 4, G11, p253* Newly renovated rooms, decked out in bright colours with lots of little mirrors and knick-knacks to make it feel more like home. En suite bathrooms and triples are also available.

E **Hostal Bergantín**, C Victoria 1, 4°, **T** 91 521 31 15, **F** 91 523 25 20, www.hostalbergantin.com *Metro Sol. Map 4, D8, p253* On a lively street in the Santa Ana area, this offers crisply furnished traditional rooms and is perfectly located for the nightlife. If you choose a balcony room bring earplugs or stay out very, very late. All rooms have bathrooms and TV.

E **Hostal Cervantes**, C Cervantes 34, **T** 91 429 83 65, **F** 91 429 27 45, www.hostal-cervantes.com *Metro Antón Martín. Map 4, E11, p253* This *hostal* is a big favourite because the friendly owners have made it feel like a home away from home. There's a cosy lounge, each room has been decorated with pretty blue prints and all have en suite bathrooms.

E **Hostal Dulcinea**, C Cervantes 19, **T** 91 429 93 09, **F** 91 369 25 69. *Metro Antón Martín. Map 4, E10, p253* Right at the top of a renovated old building, this is a very charming *hostal*. The best rooms have balconies with views out across the rooftops.

E **Hostal Gonzalo**, C Cervantes 34 3°, **T** 91 429 27 14, **F** 91 420 20 07. *Metro Antón Martín. Map 4, E11, p253* Spotless small *pensión* in a quiet location run by an extremely friendly family. Rooms have been recently redecorated and most are en suite.

E **Hostal Jaén**, C Cervantes 5, **T** 91 429 48 58, **F** 91 429 48 58, www.hjaen.com *Metro Antón Martín. Map 4, E10, p253* This *hostal* is a little more plush than the usual bare bones style and the owners are very helpful. It's located on a quiet street and, best of

all, it offers three apartments at very good rates (apartments from
€60 per night).

**E Hostal La Perla Austriana**, Plaza Santa Cruz 3, **T** 91 366 46 00,
**F** 91 366 46 08, perlaasturiana@mundivia.es *Metro Sol*. *Map 6, B6,*
*p256* Plenty of good old-fashioned Spanish kitsch at this friendly
*hostal*; plants, knick-knacks and slightly ramshackle furniture.

**E Hostal López**, C Huertas 54, **T** 91 429 43 49, **F** 91 369 47 23,
hostel@retemail.es *Metro Antón Martín*. *Map 4, F11, p253* Very
popular *hostal*, with basic but clean rooms (some triples) and very
friendly service. The best rooms have balconies onto the street
below. Budget rooms without en suite bathrooms.

**E Hostal Plaza d'Ort**, Plaza del Ángel 13, **T** 91 429 90 41, **F** 91
420 12 97, info@plazadort.com *Metro Sol*. *Map 4, E8, p253* Right
next door to the bigger and better known *Persal* (see above), this
good-value *hostal* makes a point of offering exceptionally good
service in order to compete. Rooms are decorated in typical *hostal*
chintz, but are well-equipped with TV and video, as well as a/c.

**F Hostal Bruña**, C Moratín 50, **T** 91 429 47 01. *Metro Antón
Martín*. *Map 4, E11, p253* A friendly, family-run place, it's handily
located for the Prado and Santa Ana's nightlife. Clean, spacious
whitewashed rooms with dark, wooden furniture.

**F Hostal Fonda Horizonte**, C Atocha 28, 2º B, **T** 91 369 09 96,
www.hostalhorizonte.com *Metro Antón Martín*. *Map 4, F9,*
*p253* Run by a delightful brother-and-sister team, Julio and
María-Begoña, this is a friendly small *hostal* offering charming
rooms with and without bathrooms. The best is room 8, with a
plant-filled balcony; room 15 is quiet, with a wonderful canopied
bed and a large bathroom.

**F Hostal Mirentxu**, C Zorilla 7, **T** 91 429 81 84, hmirentxu@worldonline.es *Metro Sevilla. Map 4, C11, p253* Sweet, old-fashioned *hostal* stuffed with leather sofas and knick-knacks. Rooms are excellent value; even the immaculate en suite rooms fall into this price bracket. Those without bathrooms cost considerably less.

**F Hostal Rivera**, C Atocha 79, **T** 91 429 61 30, hostalrivera@arrakis.es *Metro Antón Martín. Map 4, G11, p253* Pleasant *hostal* with simple rooms furnished in polished wood and painted in soft colours. Prices (at the very bottom of this category) are very good value for the facilities which include en suite bathrooms and TV.

**F Hostal Valencia**, C Espoz y Mina 7, **T** 91 521 18 45. *Metro Sol. Map 4, D8, p253* Small, friendly *hostal* which is geared towards younger travellers and has extras like a fridge and washing machine available for guests. All rooms are en suite and brightly decorated.

# Plaza Mayor and Los Austrias

### Hotels

**A Tryp Ambassador**, Cuesta de Santo Domingo 5, **T** 91 541 67 00, **F** 91 559 10 40, www.tryp.es *Metro Opera. Map 4, B3, p253* A chain, but set in the magnificent former palace of the Duques de Granada. Many of the original fittings have been retained, although the well-equipped rooms are blandly decorated in universal chain hotel style.

**B Los Condes**, C Los Libreros 7, Madrid, **T** 91 521 5455, **F** 91 521 7882, info@hotel-loscondes.com *Metro Callao. Map 4, A5, p252* Set in a quiet street lined with bookshops, this is a handsome hotel set in a turn-of-the-20th-century building. Rooms are comfortably, if rather fussily, decorated and prices are very good for the amenities. Affiliated with the Best Western, although independently owned and operated.

**B Santo Domingo**, Plaza Santo Domingo 13, **T** 91 547 98 00, **F** 91 547 59 95, www.hotelsantodomingo.com *Metro Santo Domingo. Map 4, A4, p252* This 16th-century mansion used to be the headquarters of the Inquisition, which should give your dreams an odd twist. It's now an elegant hotel, affiliated with Best Western, but still offers personal service and individually decorated rooms with plenty of swathed chintz. Some rooms have hydromassage baths.

**D HH Campomanes**, C Campomanes 4, **T** 91 548 85 48, www.hhcampomanes.com *Metro Opera. Map 4, B4, p252* A far cry from the pseudo-rustic theme of most small hotels; this boasts ultra-slick minimalist decor throughout, charming staff, perfect central location and a very reasonable price. Highly recommended.

## Hostales

**D Hostal Gran Duque**, C Campomanes, 6-3º, **T** 91 540 04 13, **F** 91 540 06 11, info@hostalgranduque.com *Metro Opera. Map 4, B4, p252* Newly renovated small hotel with traditionally decorated, comfortable rooms, all with en suite bathrooms. On a quiet street very close to the Opera.

**D Hostal La Macarena**, Cava de San Miguel 8, **T** 91 365 92 21, **F** 91 364 27 57. *Metro Opera. Map 6, C3, p256* Sitting right opposite a stretch of the old city walls, and surrounded by old taverns, this is set in a charming 19th-century building. Run by a friendly family, the rooms are pretty basic; it's worth noting that those overlooking the lively street are double-glazed.

**E  Hostal Pinariega**, C Santiago 1, **T** 629 351 554, **F** 629 345 116, pinariega@hostalpinariega.com  *Metro Opera.  Map 6, B2, p256*  This gem of a *hostal* is tastefully decorated with antiques and unusual artworks. Rooms with and without bathrooms. Excellent value and charming service.

**E  Hostal Valencia**, Plaza de Oriente 23, **T** 91 559 84 50. *Metro Opera.  Map 4, C2, p252*  Incomparable views over the Plaza de Oriente towards the Palacio Real, and a charming welcome from the owner, an ex-ballerina. Rooms are basic, with old-fashioned decor, but spotlessly clean.

**F  Hostal Conchita**, C Preciados 33, **T** 91 522 49 23, and **Hostal Conchita II**, C Campomanes 10, **T** 91 547 50 61. *Metro Santo Domingo.  Map 4, B4, p252*  Recently completely refurbished, both are remarkably good value and centrally located. Rooms have bathrooms and fridges. An excellent choice for budget travellers.

**G  Los Amigos**, C Campomanes 6, **T** 91 547 17 07, www.los amigoshostel.com  *Metro Opera.  Map 4, B4, p252*  New backpackers' *hostal* in a perfect, central location offering 4- or 6-person dorms; prices are €17 per person. Internet.

# La Latina and Lavapiés

## Hotels

**D  Puerta de Toledo**, Glorieta Puerta de Toledo 4, **T** 91 474 71 00. *Metro Puerta de Toledo.  Map 2, H2, p248*  Another of the dated, utterly Spanish hotels which sprang up in the 1960s and 1970s. This is staffed by important-looking men with big moustaches, which adds to the sense of going back in time. Rooms have been modernised and are sleek, quiet and well-equipped.

## Hostales

**E  Hostal El Barco**, C Mesón de Paredes 9, **T** 91 539 80 66. *Metro Tirso de Molina*. *Map 4, G6, p252*  A small, perfectly adequate cheapie tucked away on a quiet street. Rooms are basic but spotlessly clean – the best have balconies overlooking the street. Good for the alternative nightlife of La Latina and Lavapiés.

**F  Hostal Zabala**, C Magdalena 21, **T/F** 91 369 19 88, hostalzabala@wanadoo.es *Metro Antón Martín*. *Map 4, F8, p253*  Immaculate *hostal* with simple rooms which are small even by Madrid's poky standards; bathrooms are a decent size, however.

# Gran Vía, Chueca and Malasaña

## Hotels

**B  Emperador**, Gran Vía 53, **T** 91 547 2800, **F** 91 547 2817, hemperador@sei.es *Metro Callao*. *Map 4, A5, p252*  A very popular centrally located hotel with elegant original fittings and a stunning rooftop pool, open to non-guests for €25.

**C  Tryp Centro Norte**, C Mauricio Ravel 10, **T** 91 733 34 00, **F** 91 314 6047. *Metro Charmartín*.  Huge business hotel right by Chamartín train station. With excellent weekend deals, it is the cheapest you'll find if you want a pool.

**C-D  Mesón Casón del Tormes**, C del Rió 7, **T** 91 541 97 46, **F** 91 541 18 52. *Metro Plaza de España*. *Map 2, D2, p248*  Part of the Best Western chain and completely renovated in 2001. It's perfectly adequate in a bland, chain hotel sort of way, but it merits a special mention for its quiet location; a rarity in noisy Madrid. It also has excellent weekend deals and special offers.

**D  Monaco**, C Barbieri 5, **T** 91 522 4639, **F** 91 521 1601. *Metro Chueca. Map 4, A10, p253*  This enjoyably louche former brothel is now distinctly shabby, even dilapidated, but still worth checking out. To really soak up the atmosphere, ask for room 20 or room 123.

---

## Hostales

**D  Hostal Splendid**, Gran Vía 15, **T** 91 522 47 37, **F** 91 522 47 36, www.hostalsplendid.com *Metro Gran Vía. Map 4, B8, p253*
Named with reference to its magnificent, belle époque building with a beautiful wrought-iron staircase in which it's housed rather than the run-of-the-mill rooms (singles, doubles and triples). Still, all have en suite bathrooms, TV and a/c and the views of the Gran Vía's florid architecture are magnificent.

**E  Hostal Alistana**, C Hortaleza, 28, T91 521 95 18, hostalalistana @terra.es *Metro Gran Vía. Map 4, A9, p253*  Good location and low prices on this busy, buzzy Chueca street. Perfect location for the dozens of surrounding bars and restaurants.

**E  Hostal Amberes**, Gran Vía 68, **T** 91 547 61 00, **F** 91 547 61 04, info@h-amberes.com *Metro Plaza de España. Map 4, A5, p252*
The service belies the low prices; each of the pleasantly unfussy rooms is individually decorated, there's room service and a café (both 24-hour). Triples available.

**E  Hostal La Fontana**, C Valverde 6, 1°, **T** 91 523 15 61, **F** 91 521 84 49. *Metro Gran Vía. Map 4, A8, p253*  A pleasant little *hostal* with tiny rooms painted a sunny primrose. The best have flower-filled balconies.

**E  Hostal Hispano Argentino**, Gran Vía 15, 6°, **T** 91 532 24 48, **F** 91 531 72 56, info@hispano-argentino.com *Metro Gran Vía. Map 4, B9, p253*  Stuffed with knick-knacks and plants, this cheerful *hostal* with helpful staff is located in a beautiful 19th-century building on the Gran Vía. Rooms have bright bed covers, plenty of prints and dried flowers. Triples are also available.

**E Hostal Lauria**, Gran Vía 50, **T** 91 541 91 82, hostallauria@eresmas.com *Metro Callao. Map 4, A5, p252* Friendly staff and a great location; the views from the sitting room are amazing. The best rooms (all with bathrooms) face out and also have extraordinary views.

**E Hostal Marsella**, C Pez 19, **T** 91 531 47 44, **F** 91 524 13 03. *Metro Noviciado. Map 2, D4, p248* Bright, colourfully decorated rooms, most with en suite bathrooms and TV, eager-to-please staff, and a cheerfully chaotic atmosphere. An excellent budget choice and excellent value.

**F Pensión Antonio**, C Palma 62, **T** 91 532 12 93, **F** 91 523 28 23. *Metro Noviciado. Map 2, C3, p248* Good value cheapie (triples €36) in a great spot for the nightlife of Malasaña. The interior rooms are dark and poky; ask for one with a balcony onto the street.

**F–G Hostal Tokio**, C Pueblo 6, 1º, **T** 91 522 9514, hostaltokio@ole.com *Metro Gran Vía. Map 2, D4, p248* Cheerful, chaotic backpackers' *hostal*, with friendly staff and good value singles, doubles and triples.

**G Hostal Benamar**, C San Mateo 20, **T** 91 308 00 92, benamar@nexo.es *Metro Tribunal. Map 5, H1, p254* Popular backpackers' standby, with basic double and triple rooms at €14 per person. Helpful, laid-back staff.

# Salamanca and Paseo Castellano

## Hotels

**AL  Orfila**, C Orfila 6, **T** 91 702 77 70, **F** 91 702 77 72,
www.hotelorfila.com *Metro Alonso Martínez.  Map 5, E7, p255*
Converted from a luxurious 19th-century mansion, this hotel offers
discreet five-star luxury (it's part of the prestigious Relais and
Chateaux group) and has just 28 rooms and four suites, all
decorated individually in a modern take on 19th-century style.
There's a beautiful, flower-scented terrace, a charming salón de té,
and a renowned restaurant. One of the most charming hotels in the
city.

**AL  Santa Mauro**, C Zurbano 36, **T** 91 319 69 00, **F** 91 308 54 77,
www.ac-hoteles.com *Metro Gregorio Marañón.  Map 5, B7, p255*
This is a favourite with visiting celebrities who want to avoid the
public gaze. Each room in this charming 19th-century mansion has
been individually decorated, many in a slick, minimalist style.
Beautiful public areas with plump sofas and antique fireplaces,
tree-filled gardens and a large pool. There's a handsome restaurant
set in the former library.

**B  Alcalá**, C Alcalá 66, **T** 91 435 10 60, **F** 91 435 11 05. *Metro
Retiro.  Map 3, A7, p251*  Close to the Parque del Retiro, this large,
elegant hotel with a pretty interior courtyard and fresh, modern
rooms; some are decorated by Spanish designer Agatha Ruiz de la
Prada, whose trademark is bright colours and child like prints.

**B  Don Pío**, Av Pío XII 25, **T** 91 353 07 80, **F** 91 353 07 81. *Metro Pío
XII.  Map 2, C9, p249*  Close to the Ventas bullring, this modern
hotel offers all kinds of facilities for business travellers, and some
interesting extras like hydromassage baths. It sometimes offers

good weekend deals, and is a little out of town, so it's cheaper than most four-star hotels in the city.

**B  Emperatriz**, C López de Hoyos 4, **T** 91 563 80 88, **F** 91 563 98 04, www.hotel-emperatriz.com  *Metro Gregorio Marañón*.  *Map 2, A8, p249*  Set on a quiet street, this smart hotel offers spacious, luxurious rooms, many with large balconies. Personal service and excellent facilities, including a hairdressers. At the top end of this price bracket, but look out for special weekend deals.

**B  Galiano**, C Alcalá Galiano 6, **T** 91 319 2000, **F** 91 319 99 14, www.hotelgaliano.com  *Metro Colón*.  *Map 5, E8, p255*  Delightful, antique-filled hotel housed in a former palace, with spacious rooms and a leafy, central location.

**C  Residencia de El Viso**, C Nervión 8, **T** 91 564 03 70, **F** 91 564 19 65. *Metro República Argentina*.  *Map 2, A8, p249*  This pretty, pink hotel was built in the 1930s and is located in a quiet residential area. There are just a dozen rooms, which have all been completely modernised and are simple, if a little small. There's a delightful garden and a fine restaurant.

## Hostales

**C  Hostal Residencia Don Diego**, Velázquez 45, **T** 91 435 07 60, **F** 91 431 42 63. *Metro Velázquez*.  *Map 5, D12, p255*  An elegant, three-star *hostal* on a smart shopping street in the heart of Salamanca; modern, spacious rooms with polished wooden floors, all with bathrooms and satellite TV. There's also a café-bar.

Eating and drinking

Madrid, as you would expect from a major European capital, offers a huge choice of restaurants serving regional dishes from all over Spain, as well as everything from Argentine steaks to Japanese sushi. The tapas bars and restaurants in each of Madrid's neighbourhoods reflect the distinct atmosphere of the *barrios*. While there isn't much around the Paseo del Prado, the streets around the Plaza Santa Ana – just five minutes' walk from the Prado – are densely packed with all kinds of bars and restaurants. This area is a great place for the *tapeo* – the pub crawl from tapas bar to tapas bar. There are lots of traditional restaurants around the Plaza Mayor (although it's best to avoid the touristy ones on the square itself), as well as excellent gourmet tapas bars, a relatively recent phenomenon. Some of the cheapest and best tapas bars can be found in the traditionally poorer neighbourhoods of La Latina and Lavapiés, which have an appealing mixture of old-fashioned eating places and new, hip, small tapas bars and cafés, particularly on the delightful Plaza de la Paja.

### € Eating codes

**Price**

€€€ €40 and over

€€ €20-40

€ €20 and under

Prices refer to the cost of a three-course meal for one plus one glass of wine. Reservations are essential for virtually every restaurant featured, especially at weekends.

Trendy, youthful Chueca and Malasaña have better bars and clubs than restaurants, but you'll find everything from cheap, late-night places full of teenagers eating *bocadillos*, as well as dozens of stylish, more expensive places to eat. Some of the most fashionable places are restaurant, café, bar and club in one.

Salamanca is very swish and this is where Madrid's very best restaurants are tucked away. If you've got a fortune to blow on dinner, this is the place to come. It's also a good place for tapas in designer bars, but there are few places for anyone on a budget. Finally, remember that many of the bars in Madrid are cafés, tapas bars and drinking bars all rolled into one; we have only listed them once, under whichever heading we think seems most appropriate.

Eating out in Madrid is much cheaper than in most European capitals, and the very sensible tradition of the fixed-price lunch menu, the *menú del día*, means that it's possible to try out some of the city's best restaurants for a reasonable price.

Madrileños eat breakfast on the run, usually a milky coffee and a pastry at around 0730. They might leave the office for a plate of *churros* (curls of fried doughnut-like batter) dipped in a thick hot chocolate at around 1000. Lunch is eaten late, usually around 1430, with perhaps some tapas after work at around 1900. Dinner is rarely eaten before 2200, which can take some getting used to.

# Paseo del Prado and around

## Restaurants

**€€€  Viridiana**, C Juan de Mena 14, **T**   91 523 44 78.  *Metro Banco de España. Closed Sun, holidays and Aug.  Map 3, C2, p250*  A survivor from the *Movida* years, this is one of Madrid's most chic and slickest restaurants – with prices to match. Abraham García's imaginative Spanish cuisine is justly renowned, as is the excellent wine list.

**€€  Babel**, C Montalbán 9, **T** 91 521 02 77.  *Metro Banco de España. Closed Sat lunchtimes and Sun.  Map 3, C2, p250*  A welcoming, traditional restaurant specializing in chargrilled meats. Its *revueltos* – scrambled eggs with an assortment of fillings – melt in the mouth.

**€€  Paradis Casa-América**, Paseo de Recoletos 2, **T** 91 575 45 40.  *Metro Banco de España. Closed Sat lunchtimes, Sun and holidays.  Map 3, B1, p250*  Located in the Palacio de Linares (see p84), this attractive, tiled restaurant with a leafy summer terrace is a favourite with business people at lunchtimes, when it serves a good value *menú del día*. Rice dishes are the house speciality.

**€  La Fromagerie**, C Salustiano Olózaga 5, **T** 91 431 95 19. *Metro Retiro or Banco de España. Closed Aug, evenings and weekends.  Map 3, A2, p250*  Typical, old-fashioned basement Madrileño bar, serving a good value *menú del día* to local office workers.

**€  La Vaca Argentina**, C Prim 13, **T** 91 523 52 70.  *Metro Banco de España. Daily, all day.  Map 5, H6, p254*  Popular chain of Argentine restaurants, for meat-lovers only. Modern decor of the bleached wood and chrome kind.

## ▶ Local specialities

The Spanish in general and Madrileños in particular don't turn their noses up at any part of an animal; a local speciality is *callos a la madrileño*, a tripe dish cooked in a spicy tomato sauce. *Orejas* (pigs' ears) *sesos* (brains), *rinoñes* (kidneys) and even *criadillas* (bulls' testicles) feature on many menus. If you head out to Segovia, be sure to try *cochinillo*, roast suckling pig. There are hundreds of varieties of ham, from the finest *jamón ibérico*, made from pigs raised on a diet of acorns, to *jamón serrano*, cured ham. Perhaps surprisingly, given its distance from the sea, Madrid is proud of its seafood, which is shipped in freshly every day.

Most bars offer a decent variety of tapas. *Croquetas* with tuna, chicken, ham or cheese and *empanadas*, pies filled with anything from tuna to spinach. Try *boquerones*, pickled fresh anchovies, which are especially good with vermut; *patatas bravas*, fried potatoes served with a spicy sauce, and *albóndigas*, meatballs.

Wine is very popular in Madrid, and there are hundreds of wine bars offering excellent selections of wines. Good wines include the reds from Navarra, La Rioja or Ribera del Duero; the refreshing Catalan champagne, *cava*, is especially delicious on a hot day. For an *aperitivo*, try *vermut* (vermouth), a delicious, chilled, fortified wine which is best tasted fresh from the barrel.

---

## Tapas bars

**La Tapería del Prado**, Plaza de Platerías Martínez 1, **T** 91 429 40 94. *Metro Atocha or Banco de España. Daily. Map 5, E12, p253* Unusual, modern tapas in an equally modern bar overlooking a pretty square. Wild mushrooms, platters of farmhouse cheeses and inventive sandwiches.

**La Platería**, C Moratín 49, **T** 91 429 17 22. *Metro Atocha or Banco de España. Open until 0200. Map 5, E12, p253* A relaxed, stylish tapas bar overlooking a small square right across from the Prado. It's enormously popular so get there early if you want a seat on the shady terrace.

---

### Cafés

**Café Botánico**, C Ruiz de Alarcón 27. *Metro Banco de España. 1100-2200. Map 3, F2, p250* Just behind the Prado and a step away from the botanic gardens, this relaxed café-bar has tables outside on the pavement in summer.

**Hotel Ritz**, Plaza de la Lealtad 5, **T** 91 521 28 57. *Metro Banco de España. Open for breakfast 0730-1100, tea 1630-1930, drinks and tapas 1930-0100. Map 3, D1, p250* Treat yourself to tea at the Ritz; sink into a plush wicker chair in the enclosed gardens and forget the hoi polloi outside.

# Sol, Huertas and Santa Ana

---

### Restaurants

€ **La Biotika**, C Amor de Dios 3, **T** 91 429 07 80. *Metro Antón Martín. 1300-1630 and 2030-2430. Map 5, F10, p253* Bright and airy café serving tasty vegetarian food, with plenty of dishes featuring seitan and tofu. *Menú del día* only €7.50.

€ **Casa Matute**, Plaza Matute 5, **T** 91 429 43 84. *Metro Sevilla. Daily. Map 5, F9, p253* Charming, traditional Madrileño restaurant, decorated with antiques and lace curtains, which is very popular with locals. There's a good tapas bar at the front if you just want to snack.

★ **Menú del día**

B
e
s
t

- Terramundi, Santa Ana, p135
- El Txoko, Sol, Santa Ana, p136
- La Musa Latina, La Latina, p144
- Bluefish, Gran Vía, p148
- La Isla del Tesoro, Gran Vía, p149

€ **Champañería Gala**, C Moratín 22, **T** 91 429 25 62. *Metro Antón Martín. 1330-1700 and 2100-0200. Map 4, G11, p253* Valencian rice dishes, including fantastic paella, served in a beautiful, glassy patio filled with plants and flowers. *Menú del día* is excellent value.

€ **Doner Kebab Istanbul**, C Atocha. *Metro Antón Martín. 1200-2400, Fri and Sat 1200-0200. Map 2, H6, p248* It's not often you find a kebab shop with colourful turn-of-the-century tiles, marble-topped tables and chandeliers; also serves decent falafal.

€ **Gula Gula**, C Infante 5, **T** 91 420 29 19. *Metro Antón Martín. Mon-Thu 1230-1600 and 2000-2400, Fri-Sat 1230-1600 and 2000-0200, Sun 2000-2400. Map 4, H12, p253* Hip, modern restaurant tucked down a sidestreet serving buffet-style lunches plus à la carte options in the evening. The food is great and reasonably priced, but it's the crazy drag-queen cabaret acts in the evenings which are the big draw. Another, larger branch is at Gran Vía 1.

€ **Terramundi**, C Lope de Vega 32, **T** 91 429 52 80. *Metro Antón Martín. Tue-Sun 1330-1600 and 2000-2400. Map 4, F11, p253* Airy, Galician restaurant decorated with pale wood and check tablecloths, which prides itself on its homemade cooking. The accent is on seafood and there's a good value *menú del día* at €8.50.

*Eating and drinking*

135

€ **El Txoko**, C Jovellanes 3, **T** 91 532 34 43. *Metro Banco de España. Tue-Sat 1200-2300, Sun 1200-1500. Food served from 1400. Map 4, C11, p253* Basque cuisine is celebrated throughout Spain, and the basement of the Euskal Etxea (Basque Cultural Centre) is a great place for a delicious, budget lunch (*menú del día* €8), or some *pinxos* – pieces of French bread with toppings – at the bar. For a real splurge, go upstairs to the first-floor restaurant, *Erroto-Zar*.

€ **La Vaca Veronica**, C Moratín 38, **T** 91 429 78 27. *Metro Antón Martín. Mon-Fri and Sun 1400-1600 and 2100-2400, Sat 2100-2400. Map 4, F11, p253* Primrose yellow walls and chandeliers at this intimate restaurant. Mediterranean-style dishes include good grilled fish and meat, some pasta dishes and very tasty homemade desserts.

## Tapas bars

**Bar Manolo**, C Jovellanes 7, **T** 91 521 45 26. *Metro Antón Martín. 0830-2400, closed Sun and Mon evening. Map 4, C11, p253* This old-fashioned local just behind the *Cortes* and in front of the Teatro de Zarzuela is a big favourite with local politicians and journalists, who huddle together in the charming little dining room at the back. The *croquetas* are among the best in the city.

**Las Bravas**, C Espoz y Mina 13, **T** 91 532 2620. *Metro Sol. 1100-1530 and 1930-2400. Map 4, D8, p253* This is the home of *patatas bravas*: fried potatoes served with a (patented) sickly pinkish sauce. Neon-lit and garish, it's strictly for fast-food lovers but the elderly waiters in their orange overalls are a cheerful bunch. Four branches, all within a few metres of each other.

**Casa Alberto**, C Huertas 18, **T** 91 429 93 56, www.casaalberto.es *Metro Antón Martín. 1300-2400. Map 4, F8, p253* Established in 1827, nothing much has changed at this steadfastly traditional tapas bar and restaurant. Friendly waiters in long white aprons scuttle efficiently between low wooden tables, and the walls are covered in kitsch paintings and old black-and-white photos of football teams and matadors. The house speciality is *cazuela rabo de toro*, or oxtail stew; the *albondigas*, or meatballs, are also highly recommended.

**Cervecería Alemana**, Plaza Santa Ana 6, **T** 91 429 70 33. *Metro Sol. Mon, Wed, Thu and Sun 1100-2430, Fri-Sat 1100-0200. Map 4, E8, p253* An old-fashioned tapas bar with wooden tables, lace curtains and plenty of hanging hams. Go for the atmosphere rather than the slightly overpriced food.

**Cervecería La Moderna**, Plaza Santa Ana 12, **T** 91 420 1582. *Metro Sol. Mon-Thu 1200-2430. Map 4, E8, p253* Most of the bars around here cultivate an olde worlde charm, but *La Moderna* is unabashedly bright and modern. A great selection of wines and tasty, high quality tapas; try the marinated artichokes or the platter of farmhouse cheeses. Summer terrace overlooking the square.

**La Fábrica**, C Jesús 2, **T** 91 369 06 71. *Metro Antón Martín. 1100-0100. Map 4, F11, p253* A cheerful, down-to-earth locals' bar with bright orange walls and a massive range of tapas. The counters groan with a dizzying array of canapés, slices of French bread loaded with all kinds of toppings from smoked salmon to cheese and quince jelly, and an octopus steams away on top of the counter.

**Taberna Las Dolores**, Plaza de Jesús 4, **T** 91 429 22 43. *Metro Antón Martín. Open until 0100. Map 4, F11, p253* Beautiful, century-old tiled tapas bar – one of the most *típico* in the city, and always jam-packed.

## Cafés

**Café Salón del Prado**, C Prado 4, **T** 91 429 33 61. *Metro Sol. Open until 0200. Map 4, E10, p253* Elegant, spacious café full of mirrors and potted palms. Classical music concerts on Thursday evenings.

**Miau**, Plaza Santa Ana 6, **T** 91 429 22 72. *Metro Sol. 0930-2400. Map 4, E8, p253* Right on the square, with a few tables out on the pavement, this is a strange mix of old and new. Good for breakfast, as it's one of the few places in this area to open early.

**La Luiza**, Plaza Santa Ana 2, **T** 91 521 08 11. *Metro Sol. Mon-Thu 0700-2400, Fri-Sat 0800-0200, Sun 0800-2400. Map 4, E9, p253* Delightful, old-fashioned pastry shop with just a few tables. A great place for breakfast – a creamy *café con leche* and a sweet croissant or *ensaïmada*.

**Sherazade**, C Santa María 6. *Metro Antón Martín. 2000-0300, until 0430 Fri-Sat. Map 4, F11, p253* Step into this Moroccan tearoom through the horseshoe arch doorway and sink languidly onto a low stool or a pile of cushions. Cocktails and tea are served.

# Plaza Mayor and Los Austrias

## Restaurants

€€€ **Al Norte**, C San Nicolás 8, **T** 91 547 22 22. *Metro Opera. Closed Sun evening. Map 4, D2, p252* Ultra-modern, sleek new restaurant, serving specialities from Spain's Atlantic coast, with plenty of deliciously fresh seafood and vegetables. *Menú del día* at around €12 and a fine wine list. There's a shady terrace, too.

★ **For breakfast**

**Best**

- Bluefish, Gran Vía, p148
- La Luiza, Santa Ana, p138
- Café Oliver, Gran Vía, p165
- Café de los Austrias, p142

€€€ **La Taberna del Alaberdero**, C Felipe V, **T** 91 541 51 92. *Metro Opera. 1300-1600, 2100-2400*. *Map 4, B3, p252* Just off the Plaza de Oriente, with a small *terraza* in summer, this celebrated restaurant serves exquisite Basque cuisine; splash out on the five-course *menú de degustación*. A wide variety of tapas and *raciones* are available in the bar.

€€ **Casa Botín**, C Cuchilleros 17, **T** 91 366 42 17. *Metro Sol. 1300-1600 and 2000-2400*. *Map 6, D4, p256* This rambling, stone-built restaurant tucked into what was once the city walls is the oldest restaurant in Madrid (founded in 1725). It's touristy, but it's still one of the best places to try the Madileño speciality of *cochinillo*, or roast suckling pig.

€€ **Casa Paco**, Plaza Puerta Cerrada 11, **T** 91 366 31 66. *Metro La Latina. Mon-Sat 1330-1600 and 2030-2400, closed Sun*. *Map 6, E3, p256* A resolutely old-fashioned tiled bar with a restaurant at the back. Dignified waiters in long aprons serve traditional sizzling grilled meats, accompanied by a good selection of Spanish wines. Black-and-white photographs show the founder posing with everyone from Catherine Deneuve to the King of Spain. Simple tapas are available at the bar.

**Eating and drinking**

€€ **Cornucopia**, C Flora 1, **T** 91 547 64 65. *Metro Opera. Tue-Sun 1330-1630. Map 4, C5, p252* Tucked away in an old mansion, this colourful, quirky restaurant is a real find: sunshine-yellow walls, a deep blue ceiling, changing art exhibits, crisp white tablecloths, and fresh flowers on the tables. Spanish-American owned, it serves modern European food (always a vegetarian choice), and sublime desserts; don't miss the strawberry mousse. *Menú del día* costs €10.

€€ **Entre Suspiro y Suspiro**, C Caños de Peral **T** 91 542 06 44. *Metro Opera. Mon-Fri 1400-1630 and 2130-2330, Sat 2130-2330. Map 4, B4, p252* Romantic, family-run Mexican restaurant just off the Plaza Isabel II, decorated with a profusion of plants and ceramics, serving genuine and delicious Mexican cuisine made with the freshest ingredients.

€€ **Verde Oliva**, C Segovia 8, **T** 91 541 35 40. *Metro La Latina. Mon-Fri 1300-1600 and 2100-0100, until 0200 on Sat, Sun 1300-1700. Map 6, E, p246* New, fashionable spot designed by the cinematographer Julio Torrecillas, scattered with paintings and sculptures. Olive oil is king, and the dishes include risotto with wild mushrooms and pistachios and wok-fried vegetables.

## Tapas bars

**El Barandal**, C Independencia 2, **T** 91 541 11 33. *Metro Opera. 1700-0130. Closed Mon and Aug. Map 4, C3, p252* Tasty tapas (in minuscule portions) are served at this delightful, ochre-painted bar overlooked by a small wrought-iron gallery (or verandah) which gives the place its name. Dining area at the back.

**El Púlpito**, Plaza Mayor 10. *Metro Sol. 0930-0100. Map 6, C4, p256* Tiny, brightly-lit bar tucked away in the corner of the square which serves all kinds of tapas; try the grilled prawns.

★ **Best**

**Vegetarian joints**

- La Biotika, Santa Ana, p134
- Cornucopia, Plaza Mayor, p140
- El Estragón, La Latina, p144
- Elquí, La Latina, p143
- La Isla del Tesoro, Gran Vía, p149

**La T de San Miguel**, Plaza del Conde de Miranda 4, **T** 91 559 98 19. *Metro Opera or Sol. Map 6, C2, p256* A newish basement tapas bar and restaurant which combines old brick and shiny chrome by the Mercado San Miguel. Also good for a reasonably priced dinner.

**Taberna del Cruzado**, C Amnistía 8, **T** 91 548 0131. *Metro Opera. 1300-1600, 2000-2400, until 0030 Fri and Sat, closed Tue evening. Map 4, C3, p252* This has a beautiful carved wooden bar, dark red and cream walls, and charming staff. Among the unusual tapas are fried oyster mushrooms served with *aïoli*, a creamy garlic dip.

**Taberna Miranda**, Plaza Donde Miranda 4, **T** 91 541 37 00. *Metro Opera. Tue-Fri 0900-1630 and 2000-2400, Sat and Sun 2000-2400. Map 6, C2, p256* Spacious, low-lit wooden bar and restaurant with rustic decor serving a good range of tapas; the range of wines is exceptionally good.

**Taberna 4 Robles**, Plaza de Celenque 1, **T** 91 522 76 86. *Metro Opera or Sol. Map 4, C6, p252* Bright and breezy tiled Andaluz-style tapas bar – good range of tapas, including tasty *pescaditos fritos*, fried fish.

**Eating and drinking**

## Cafés

**Café de los Austrias**, Plaza de Ramales 1, **T** 91 559 84 36. *Metro Opera. Mon-Thu 0900-0130, Fri-Sat 0900-0230, Sun 0900-2400. Map 4, C2, p252* Large, old-fashioned café-bar with marble columns and mirrors which is very popular with locals. A perfect spot to while away an afternoon.

**Café de Oriente**, Plaza de Oriente 2, **T** 91 541 39 74. *Metro Opera. 0930-0130, until 0230 on Fri and Sat. Map 4, C3, p252* Famous, chic café with a large terrace overlooking the square and the Palacio Real. There's an expensive restaurant, too, if you want to splash out for a special occasion.

**Chocolatería San Ginés**, Pasadizo San Ginés. *Metro Opera. Map 4, D5, p252* Tucked down a passage off Calle Arenal, this is the classic place to finish off a night out on the town, with *churros con chocolate* at dawn.

**Inshalá**, C Amnistía 10, **T** 91 548 2632. *Metro Opera. Open until 0300 on Sat. Closed Sun. Map 4, C3, p252* Trendy, mellow Moroccan-style tearoom and bar with mosaic tables, wall hangings, lanterns and candles, and cushioned benches. Delicious couscous dishes, as well as a special from a different country each day. Live music on Fridays, *menú del día* for €7.50.

**Café La Unión**, C Unión 1, **T** 91 542 55 63. *Metro Opera. 1700-0300, until late on Fri and Sat, Sun 1700-0130. Map 4, C2, p 252* Stylish, airy café with changing art exhibitions, friendly staff and a mellow atmosphere; great place for a chat at any time. Fantastic *mojitos*, among the best in Madrid.

# La Latina and Lavapiés

## Restaurants

€€€ **Casa Lucio**, Cava Baja 35, **T** 91 365 32 52. *Metro La Latina. Closed sat lunchtimes and Aug. Map 4, G3, p252*
Celebrated typically Madrileño restaurant that is so popular it's had to open another dining area across the street. The original space is the most atmospheric; this is the place to try Madrid-style tripe or *cocido*.

€€€ **Viejo Madrid**, Cava Baja 32, **T** 91 366 83 23. *Metro La Latina. Map 4, F4, p252* Deeply traditional, romantic and cosy, this inn serves up some of the city's best food; great seafood and an extensive wine list.

€€ **Palacio de Anglona**, C Segovia 14, **T** 91 366 37 53. *Metro La Latina. 1330-1600 and 2030-0100, until 0230 Fri-Sat. Map 2, E1, p256* Fashionable, reasonably priced restaurant set in a 19th-century palace, with sleek, pared-down decor. Grilled meats, pasta dishes and unusual salads.

€ **La Burbuja que Ríe**, C Ángel 16, **T** 91 366 51 67. *Metro Puerta de Toledo. Tue 2000-2400, Wed-Sun 1300-1700 and 2000-2400. Map 4, F2, p252* Noisy, cheerful, traditional Asturian restaurant where you can watch cider being poured from shoulder-height in the traditional way. Try the hearty stews and pungent goat's cheese.

€ **Elquí**, C Buenavista 18, **T** 91 468 04 62. *Metro Antón Martín. Lunchtimes only, except at weekends, closed Mon and Aug. Map 4, H10, p253* This budget, self-service vegetarian restaurant was the first in Madrid. Very good value, if slightly lacking in atmosphere.

€ **El Estragón**, Plaza de la Paja 10, **T** 91 365 89 92. *Metro La Latina. 1330-1600 and 2000-2400. Map 4, F2, p252* Friendly, pretty vegetarian restaurant set over several levels overlooking one of Madrid's loveliest squares. The food is very creative, using unusual combinations of ingredients.

€ **Entrecajas**, C Moreria 11, **T** 91 365 12 14. *Metro La Latina. Tue-Sun 1300-late. Map 4, F1, p252* Cool, minimalist decor with plenty of dark wood and chrome; attentive, friendly staff and excellent good value Mediterranean food (with plenty of vegetarian choice), including scrumptious salads and delicious desserts.

€ **La Falsa Molestia**, C Magdalena 32, **T** 91 420 32 38, www.lafalsamolestia.com *Metro Antón Martín Closed Mon and Tue. Map 4, G8, p253* Slick, arty café-restaurant-bar serving light, fresh Italian dishes and delectable home-made desserts. Unusually, they feature a water list as well as a wine list. Laid-back chill-out music, charming (and preternaturally handsome) Italian staff, and excellent coffee – perhaps the best place to relax in the city .

€ **La Musa Latina**, Costanilla de San Andrés 12, **T** 91 354 02 55. *Metro La Latina. 1200-1600 and 1930-2400. Map 4, F2, p252* This newly opened huge, stylish restaurant-café-tapas bar is right on the delightful Plaza de la Paja and is already popular with the theatre/movie crowd. New York loft meets the Far East in the decor and the food is equally eclectic and extremely good. There's an excellent *menú del día* at €8.

€ **El Viajero**, Plaza de la Cebada 11, **T** 91 366 90 94. *Metro La Latina. Tue-Sat 1400-1630 and 2100-2430, Sun 1400-1630. Map 4, G3, p252* Enormously popular, bohemian, three-storey Argentine restaurant, with a much sought-after rooftop terrace overflowing with plants and flowers and an equally popular bar.

### ★ Tasas and tiles

**Best**

## Tapas bars

**Taberna Almendro**, C Almendro 13, **T** 91 365 42 52. *Metro La Latina. 1300-1600 and 1900-2400. Map 6, F2, p256* Old-fashioned, friendly spot with ochre walls hung with wooden racks full of sherry glasses and oak barrels for tables; house specialities include *roscas* (a round, well stuffed sandwich) and, more surprisingly, egg, bacon and chips (a great hangover cure). Excellent olives, too.

**Taberna Bilbao**, Plaza de la Paja (Costanilla de San Andrés), **T** 91 365 6125. *Metro La Latina. Tue-Sun 1300-1600, 2030-2400. Map 4, F2, p252* Large, sleek bar with brick walls, chrome furnishings and a deep orange ceiling. Friendly staff in crisp uniforms serve fresh Basque goodies like *callos a la Vizcaína* (Basque-style tripe), as well as *croquetas*, cured meats and salads. There are more than 100 wines to choose from – try the young, crisp Basque wine *Txacoli*.

**La Carpanta**, C Almendro 22, **T** 91 366 57 83. *Metro La Latina. Closed Mon and Tue mornings in summer, open until 0130, 0230 on Fri and Sat. Map 4, G3, p252* Stylish, hugely popular tapas bar with a dining area at the back, quirky wooden furnishings, paddle fans and old brick walls. It's run by a famous Madrileño family of actors.

**Casa Amadeo**, Plaza Cascorro. *Metro La Latina. Closed Sun evening. Map 4, H5, p252* This is a favourite post-Rastro haunt on a

Sunday; it's nicknamed *Los Caracoles*, for its most famous *tapa* of snails.

**Casa Montes**, C Lavapiés 40, **T** 91 527 00 64. *Metro Lavapiés. 1200-1600, 1930-2400, Sun 1200-1600. Closed Mon and Aug. Map 4, H7, p253* This tiny neighbourhood bar which hasn't changed in decades has an excellent range of wines served with tasty tapas like cured meats and farmhouse cheeses. In summer, people spill out onto the square.

**La Taberna de L'Avapiés**, C Lavapiés 5, **T** 91 539 26 50. *Metro Lavapiés. Daily 1200-1700, 1930-0200, Sun 1200-1600. Map 4, G7, p253* Laid-back neighbourhood bar with beamed ceilings, friendly staff and a good range of tapas including delicious *croquetas* and a few veggie options.

**Taberna Tempranillo**, Cava Baja 38, **T** 91 364 1532. *Metro La Latina. 1200-1600 and 1930-0200. Map 4, G3/4, p252* A paddle fan flaps lazily and there's a vast wall of wine bottles behind the bar. An excellent selection of wines, including weekly specials, and a good (if pricey) menu of cured meats and regional cheeses, including a contender for smelliest cheese ever – La Perbal from Asturias.

### Cafés

**Café Barbieri**, C Ave María 45, **T** 91 527 36 58. *Metro Lavapiés. 1500-0200, until 0300 Fri-Sat. Map 4, H8, p253* Oozing turn-of-the-20th-century charm and filled with burnished mirrors and battered wooden tables. The classical music and sheaf of newspapers make it the perfect spot to while away the afternooon.

**Champañería Librería**, Plaza Gabriel Miró 1, Las Vistillas, **T** 91 366 23 70. *Metro La Latina. 1100-2300. Map 4, F1, p253* This

**Heavenly chorizo**
*Platters like these, displaying the red coloured sausage to titillate your taste buds, decorate the windows of many a bakery and café in the streets of the city.*

relaxed café-bar is decked out like an old Parisian café, with a small library, sofa, standard lamp and piano. It gets livelier at night.

**Cine Doré**, C Santa Isabel 3, **T** 91 369 49 23. *Metro Antón Martín. 1600-2400, closed Mon. Map 4, G9, p253* This pretty café attached to the art deco cinema (see p54) has a delightful terrace where films are shown on summer evenings. Good salads and snacks.

**Paraty**, Plaza Gabriel Miró 2, **T** 91 364 15 62. *Metro La Latina. 1200-2400. Map 4, F1, p252* Simple, modern café-bar with changing art exhibitions and a buzzy young crowd in the popular Las Vistillas neighbourhood.

# Gran Vía, Chueca and Malasaña

## Restaurants

€€ **La Castafiore**, C Barquillo 30, **T** 91 532 21 00. *Metro Chueca. Mon-Sat 1300-1600 and 2130-0100. Map 5, H6, p254* Elegant and traditional, but entirely unstuffy, this charming restaurant features Basque cuisine; the food is excellent but the real draw is the waiters, who break into snatches of opera and zarzuela at weekends.

€ **Bluefish**, C San Andrés 26, **T** 91 448 67 65. *Metro Bilbao. Tue-Sat 1300-0100, Sun 0100-1800. Map 5, D1, p254* A zinc counter curves around the deep blue and scarlet bar, and the candle-lit lounge area at the back has deep, comfy seats. Delicious food (try the spinach and goat's cheese salad), an excellent value three-course *menú del día* (€8) and US-style brunches at weekends. A hip crowd come for the excellent cocktails in the evenings.

★ **Best**

**Summer terraces**

- Viva Madrid, Sol, p161
- Cervecería La Moderna, Sol, p137
- El Viajero, La Latina, p144
- Café de Oriente, Plaza Mayor, p142
- Café Gijón, Salamanca, p153

€ **La Isla del Tesoro**, C Manuel Malasaña 3, **T** 91 593 14 40. *Metro Bilbao. Closed Sun and lunchtime in holidays. Map 5, D1, p254* Exotic bamboo screens, sea shells and deep blue walls make this a wonderfully romantic spot; it's vegetarian, and the well-priced *menú del día* (€8.50) features the cuisine of a different country each day.

€ **La Mordida**, C Belén 13, **T** 91 308 20 89, www.lamordida.net *Metro Chueca or Alonso Martínez. Mon-Thu 1330-1700 and 2030-0100, Fri-Sat 2030-0300. Map 5, G5, p255* Fun, colourful and boisterous Mexican restaurant serving fine food, but it's the party atmosphere that everyone comes for.

€ **El Pepinillo de Barquillo**, C Barquillo 42, **T** 91 310 25 46. *Metro Chueca. 1300-0100. Map 5, H6, p254* Bright bar with tables covered in red-check tablecloths, serving a light menu featuring salads, seafood and grilled vegetables; a huge gherkin on a cocktail stick is suspended from the ceiling.

## Tapas bars

**Bar Casa do Compañeiro**, C San Vicente Ferrern 44, **T** 91 521 57 02. *Metro Noviciado. Map 2, C4, p248* Home to Alberto the parokeet, this is a tiled, slightly battered old tapas bar run by a friendly Galician family. There's plenty of *pulpo* (octopus) and other fish on the menu, and they also serve crisp, cold vermouth from the barrel.

**Stop Madrid**, C Hortaleza 11, **T** 91 521 88 87.   *Metro Gran Vía.   1230-1600, 1800-0200, until 0230 on Fri and Sat.   Map 4, A8, p253+*   Eccentric but stylish former *jamonería*, with a buzzy atmosphere and a few basic tapas like tortilla and olives.

**Albur**, C Manuel Malasaña 15, **T** 91 594 27 33.   *Metro Bilbao.   1230-2400.   Map 5, D1, p254*   Relaxed neighbourhood restaurant and tapas bar popular with local office workers.

**La Musa**, C Manuel Malasaña 18, **T** 91 48 75 58.   *Metro Bilbao.   0900-0030, until 0100 Fri-Sat.   Map 5, D1, p254*   Hugely popular with a young, lively crowd, this cellar tapas bar serves up excellent and imaginative tapas and *raciones*.

**Bodegas de Angel Sierra**, C Gravina 11, **T** 93 531 01 26.   *Metro Chueca.   1030-1600 and 1900-2300.   Map 5, G4, p254*   Ancient, delightfully old-fashioned bar with battered, dark wooden fittings and a marble counter; vermuouth on tap, perfectly accompanied with a *tapa* of anchovy and olive.

**El Pez Gordo**, C Pex 6, **T** 91 522 32 08.   *Metro Noviciado.   Map 5, G1, p254*   The Fat Fish (which in Spanish means something like our the Big Cheese) is a fairly ordinary tapas bar made extraordinary by its delicious food and its entertaining and theatrical clientele.

## Cafés

**Café Comercial**, Glorieta de Bilbao 7, **T** 91 521 56 55. *Metro Bilbao.   0730-0100 until 0200 Fri-Sat.   Map 5, D2, p254*   Huge, famous, scruffy old café with outdoor tables in summer, mirrors and marble-topped tables with internet upstairs.

**Café Manuela**, C San Vicente Ferrer 29, **T** 91 531 70 37. *Metro Tribunal. Mon-Thu 1800-0200, Fri-Sun 1600-0230. Map 5, F1, p254* Large, lush Art Nouveau-style café, featuring live music, story-telling evenings, poetry readings and *tertulias*.

**Café de Ruiz**, C Ruiz 11, **T** 91 446 12 32. *Metro Bilbao. 1230-0230. Map 5, D1, p254* A local institution, set in a series of small salons, with plush sofas, low lighting and dark wooden fittings. Good for cakes, coffee and cocktails.

**El Café sin Nombre**, C Conde Duque 10, **T** 91 548 09 72. *Metro Plaza de España. Mon-Fri 0930-0100, Sat 2000-0300, closed Sun. Map 2, C3, p248* A couple of sofas, regular art exhibitions and a great choice of coffee make this a good afternoon stop-off. Gets livelier at night.

**El Jardín Secreto**, C Conde Duque 2, **T** 91 541 80 23. *Metro Plaza de España. Mon-Thu 1730-0100, Fri-Sat 1800-0230, Sun 1700-2400. Map 2, C3, p248* Magical, tranquil café with rattan furniture and a scattering of shells, candles and hazy drapes. Occasionally marred by terrible music.

**Lémao**, C Infantas 4. *Metro Gran Vía. Mon-Thu 1000-2400, Fri-Sat 1000-0300, Sun 1000-1600. Map 4, A8, p253* Ultra-trendy café-bar serving light snacks like soup, salads, sandwiches, as well as vitamin-packed juices and smoothies.

## Salamanca and the Paseo Castellano

### Restaurants

€€€ **El Amparo**, C Puigcerdá, **T** 91 431 64 56. *Metro Serrano. Closed Sat lunchtimes and Sun. Map 5, G11, p255* The Basques are widely renowned for their culinary expertise and nowhere does it better than this glamorous restaurant.

€€€ **Zalacaín**, C Alvarez de Baena 4, **T** 91 561 48 40. *Metro Gregorio Marañón. Closed lunchtimes, Sun, holidays, Holy Week and Aug. Map 2, A7, p249* Madrid's most celebrated restaurant, holder of all kinds of stars and awards. Chef Benjamín Urdiaín can't put a foot wrong, it seems; cuisine, service and decor ooze elegance and assurance.

€€ **Teatriz**, C Hermosilla 15, **T** 91 577 53 79. *Metro Serrano. 1330-1600 and 2030-2300; bar open until 0200, until 0300 Fri-Sat. Map 5, E10, p255* Philip Starck and Javier Mariscal famously converted this theatre during the last years of the *Movida* and it's still a place to see and be seen. Regardless of all the hype, the Italian food is very good. Designer tapas, too.

€€ **Thai Gardens**, C Jorge Juan 5, **T** 91 577 88 84. *Metro Serrano. Open until 0100 at weekends. Map 5, G10, p255* Beautiful, deeply romantic restaurant decorated with traditional Thai crafts and silks; the finest Thai food in Madrid is on offer here.

€ **Taberna de la Daniela**, C General Pardiñas 21, **T** 91 575 23 29. *Metro Goya. 1330-1600 and 2030-2300. Map 2, C10, p249* Classic old-style tavern serving traditional Madrileño cuisine to an oddly mixed clientele of smartly dressed locals and old men propping up the bar. Excellent tapas; try the *croquetas* and *empanadas*.

## Tapas bars

**El Barril**, C Don Román de la Cruz 91, **T** 91 401 33 05. *Metro Lista. Closed second fortnight in Aug. Map 2, C10, p249* Chilled sherry served from the barrel makes an excellent accompaniment

**★ Best**

**Restaurants for a splurge**

• Viridiana, Paseo del Prado, p132
• Casa Lucio, La Latina, p143
• Al Norte, Plaza Mayor, p138
• Zalacaín, Salamanca, p152.
• El Amparo, Salamanca, p151

to the seafood specialities like *pulpo a la gallega*, octopus in a spicy tomato sauce.

**El Olivar de Ayala**, C Ayala 84, **T** 91 576 77 64. *Metro Goya. Closed Sun evening, Mon and Aug. Map 2, C10, p249* Everything is on a big scale at this spacious bar with large barrels for tables and generous portions. Good ham *croquetas* and *salmorejo* (a chilled Andaluz soup), in summer.

**La Taberna del Buey**, C General Pardiñas 7, **T** 91 578 11 54. *Metro Serrano. 1300-1600 and 1930-2400. Map 2, D10, p249* Swish, upmarket bar serving high-quality Basque tapas including *pinxos*, (bread with all kinds of toppings), and oxtail *albóndigas* (meatballs). There's also a dining area.

**Los Timbales**, C Alcalá 227, **T** 91 725 07 68. *Metro Ventas. 1300-1630 and 2000-2400. Map 2, D11, p249* Crammed with bullfighting memorabilia, this is the classic stop-off before or after a *corrida*. Good tapas, including the house speciality, *timbales* or pies stuffed with meat or cheese, and a terrace in summer.

### Cafés

**Café Gijón**, Paseo de Recoletos 21, **T** 91 521 54 25. *Metro Banco de España. 0800-0200. Map 5, H7, p254* One of the oldest and

*Eating and drinking*

loveliest cafés in Madrid, still haunted by the ghosts of 19th-century *tertulias*. Tapas, *raciones* and meals are also available.

**Chocolatería Jorge Juan**, C Jorge Juan 12, **T** 91 577 06 07. *Metro Serrano. 0800-2200. Map 5, G11, p255* After a night on the tiles, this is the best place to come for *churros con chocolate* in Salamanca.

**Embassy**, C Castellana 12, **T** 91 575 66 33. *Metro Colón. 0930-0100. Map 5, D9, p255* This chi chi delicatessen also has a delightful café where you can tuck into cakes with the ladies who lunch.

# Around Madrid

### San Lorenzo de El Escorial

€€€ **Charolés**, C Floridablanca 24, **T** 91 890 59 75. This is El Escorial's most celebrated restaurant; the Wednesday *cocido* has become an institution. Terrace in summer.

€€ **Fonda Genara**, Plaza San Lorenzo, **T** 91 890 43 57. Tucked away between two squares, this traditional restaurant serves homecooked dishes and is decorated with old photographs of the town.

€ **La Cueva**, C San Antón 4, **T** 91 890 15 16. Another popular spot, *La Cueva* is a delightfully rickety old inn set over three floors which offers tapas in the bar or tasty local dishes in the dining area.

### Segovia

€€€ **Mesón de José María**, C Cronista Lecea 11, **T** 92 146 60 17. Cándido's former pupil José María has been making a big name for himself at his own *méson*, rated as one of Segovia's best restaurants. It's a great place to try the local speciality of *cochinillo* and there's a lively bar area for tapas if you don't want a big meal.

€€ **Mesón de Cándido**, Plaza Azoguejo 5, **T** 92 142 81 03. The late Señor Cándido was a legend, and his restaurant, picturesquely huddled under the aqueduct arches, is papered with photos of famous clients. Now run by his son, its reputation has palled slightly, but it's still a memorable spot for lunch.

€ **Cuevas de San Esteban**, C Valdeláguila 15, **T** 92 146 09 82. This cavernous bar-restaurant just off the Plaza San Esteban is a big favorite with locals. Good tapas and simple meals.

## Toledo

€€€ **Asador Adolfo**, C La Granada 6, **T** 92 533 73 21. Classic Toledano restaurant serving excellent regional dishes accompanied by an equally fine wine list.

€ **La Abadía**, C Nuñez de Arce 3, **T** 92 525 11 40. This restaurant-bar is enormously popular with locals who spill out on the street with their drinks. Excellent tapas and a good value *menú del día*.

€ **Casa Ludeña**, Plaza de la Magdalena 13, **T** 92 522 33 84. A very friendly, old-fashioned restaurant serving Toledano classics like partridge or *cuchifritos* (lamb cooked in sauce of tomatoes, egg, wine and saffron). Good value *menú del día*.

## Avila

€€ **Hostería de Bracamonte**, C Bracamonte 6, **T** 92 025 12 80. Located in a beautifully restored palace, this is one of Avila's finest

Eating and drinking

restaurants; don't miss the succulent house speciality of *cordero asado* (roast lamb).

€ **Casa Patas**, C San Millán 4, **T** 92 021 31 94. A local stalwart, this old-fashioned bar serves good tapas and simple meals.

€ **Mesón del Rastro**, Plaza del Rastro 1, **T** 92 021 12 18. A traditional Castillian restaurant with dark, wooden beams serving hearty stews and grilled meats.

## Aranjuez

€€ **Asador Palacio de Osuna**, C Príncipe 21, **T** 91 892 42 15. A sumptuous restaurant set in a wing of a palace which once belonged to the Duke of Osuna.

€ **La Rana Verde**, C Reina 1, **T** 91 891 32 38. Reasonable if unexceptional food in a lovely riverside setting.

## Alacalá de Henares

€€€ **Hostería del Estudiante**, C Colegios 3, **T** 91 888 03 30. If you want to splash out, this elegant restaurant (part of Alcalá's parador) is the perfect choice.

€ **La Cúpula**, C Santiago 18, **T** 91 880 73 91. Housed in a former convent, this is the place to come for traditional local specialities, as well as meats grilled over a brazier.

Madrid's legendary nightlife may have gone off the boil since the giddy days of the *Movida*, but it's still among the best in Europe. The club scene is raging, with international DJs as well as plenty of homegrown ones, and there's something for everyone. Over the past few years the city council have been attempting to stamp out the so-called 'after hours' clubs which carried on when the regular clubs were closing their doors at dawn, but it's still possible to start dancing on Friday night and not stop until Monday morning. Most of the big clubs can be found along the Gran Vía and the Paseo Castellano, but Madrid also has hundreds of *discobares*, bars with DJs and small dance floors, spread all over the city.

Most regular bars function as cafés during the day, opening in the morning until about midnight. *Bares de copas*, drinking bars, are usually open in the evenings only from about 2100. Clubs rarely open before midnight and get going from 0100 or 0200 onwards. Clubs charge anything from €5 and €15. To get the latest, visit www.clubbinginspain.com

Around the Paseo del Prado nightlife is pretty non-existent, althought it's close to the Salamanca and Santa Ana neighbourhoods if you're looking for some fun. Santa Ana and Huertas gets packed, especially on summer nights. There are hundreds of tapas bars and fewer cocktail bars, but plenty of clubs. It's not an especially fashionable *barrio*, but you are guaranteed a good time. In the Plaza Mayor and Los Austrias area, the streets around Plaza de la Paja are packed with cool bars and fancy tapas bars and restaurants, but there's also a healthy sprinkling of down-to-earth neighbourhood bars. There are some very funky bars tucked away in the formerly run-down neighbourhoods of La Latina and Lavapiés, which are starting to attract plenty of young artists. Gran Vía, Malasaña and Chueca is where to go to party. Chueca is the heart of the gay district and stuffed with some ultra-stylish bars and cafés. Malasaña is popular with students and younger people looking for a good time. Most of the big mega-clubs can be found along the Gran Vía. Salamanca is very upmarket. No trainers and skyhigh priced drinks. The Paseo Castellana comes into its own in summer when everyone heads for the vast outdoor *terrazas*.

# Paseo del Prado and around

### Bars

**Alquimia**, C Villanueva 2, **T** 91 577 27 85.  *Metro Retiro.  2030-0500. Map 5, H8, p253*  Restaurant-bar-club combo. Hip venue. A place to lounge about in deep leather sofas or dine in faux-Gothic splendour. Wear your Manolos.

**La Divina Comedia**, C Almadén 14.  *Metro Atocha.  Wed-Sun 2100-0300, closed Mon-Tue.  Map 4, G12, p253*  Cool, candle-lit bar with deep ochre walls and lamps made from popcorn boxes. The Mexican owner mixes a mean margarita.

**Garamond**, C Claudio Coello 10, **T** 91 578 19 74. *Metro Retiro. 1800-0330, until 0430 Fri-Sat. Map 5, H9, p255* A favourite with thesps and TV celebrities, this is a chi chi cocktail bar and disco, with occasional live music.

## Clubs

**Kapital**, C Atocha 125, **T** 91 420 29 06. *Metro Atocha. Thu 2400-0700, Fri-Sun 2400-0700. Map 3, H1, p250* Huge, fun mega-club on six floors, with a rooftop terrace, cinema and karaoke bar. Early sessions are aimed at teens.

# Sol, Huertas and Santa Ana

## Bars

**Cardamomo**, C Echegaray 15, **T** 91 369 07 57. *Metro Sevilla. Tue-Sun 2100-0330. Map 4, D9, p253* Despite its dated look – all vintage posters and fake memorabilia – this is a cool spot which offers regular live music, including some excellent jazz, flamenco and salsa.

**Oui**, C Cervantes 7, **T** 91 521 84 15. *Metro Antón Martín. Wed-Sun 1900-0300, closed Mon-Tue. Map 4, E10, p253* Laid-back, low-lit lounge bar where you can chill out with a cocktail on a cushioned banquette. Regular DJs at weekends, when the bar is crammed.

**El Parnasón**, C Moratín 25, **T** 91 420 19 75. *Metro Antón Martín. Sun-Thu 2000-2430, Fri-Sat 2000-0330. Map 4, F11, p253* Dim, tiny and deeply romantic bar crammed with bizarre bric-a-brac; there's a red velvet salon at the back and the fantastic cocktails are served in goldfish bowls (well, nearly).

**Viva Madrid**, C Fernandez González 7, **T** 91 521 36 40. *Metro Sol or Sevilla. 1800-0200. Map 4, E9, p253* Huge, beautifully tiled bar on two levels, with paddle fans, simple tapas and DJ sessions at weekends. An ex-pat favourite, with a summer terrace and pricey drinks.

---

## Clubs

**La Boca del Lobo**, C Echegaray 11, **T** 91 429 70 13. *Metro Sevilla. 2200-0500. Map 4, D9, p253* Small, laid-back club where you can hear everything from trip-hop to 50s rock-and-roll. Occasional film-screenings and other events.

**Suite Café-Club**, C Virgen de los Peligros 4, **T** 91 521 40 31. *Metro Sevilla. Thu-Sat 2300-0500. Map 4, B9, p253* Plenty of film stars at this favourite restaurant-cum-bar-cum-club with the so-cool-it-hurts crowd; sharp 70s-style decor, good global fusion cuisine in the restaurant, cool ambient sounds on one dance floor and deep house on the other.

**Torero**, C Cruz 26, **T** 91 523 11 29. *Metro Sevilla. Tue-Sat 2300-0600. Map 4, D8, p253* Upmarket club for the well-heeled – no trainers – but worth the trouble of dressing up for the buzzy atmosphere.

**Villa Rosa**, Plaza Santa Ana 15, **T** 91 521 36 89. *Metro Sol or Sevilla. Mon-Sat 2300-0600. Map 4, E8, p253* Former flamenco *tablao* is covered in colourful tiles inside and out. Mixed, fun crowd and eclectic music.

# Plaza Mayor and Los Austrias

## Bars

**El 21**, C Toledo 21, **T** 91 366 28 59. *Metro Sol.  Tue-Sun 1130-1540 and 1830-2300, Sat until 0100.  Map 6, C4, p256*  Dusty old-fashioned bar with fading bullfighting posters and a crowd of elderly regulars. It's become an institution with bright young things getting ready for the long night ahead.

**El Barbú**, C Santiago 3, **T** 91 542 56 98. *Metro Opera.  Tue-Sun 2000-0100.  Map 6, B2, p256*  Low-lit, slinky café and cocktail bar popular with 30-somethings and a wonderfully romantic back room furnished with baroque sofas.

**El Cañi**, C Santiago 11, **T** 91 541 12 55. *Metro Opera.  Wed-Mon 2000-0100.  Map 6, A1, p256*  Fantastic, super-friendly neigh-bourhood bar, crammed with paintings and cartoons by the charismatic owner Julio. He and some of his regulars have formed a band, Los Lamentables, which look set to hit the big time. It's the kind of bar where anything can happen – an impromptu flamenco performance, a tap dance, or a sing-along session. Great fun.

## Clubs

**Joy Madrid**, C Arenal 11, T 91 366 54 39.  *Metro Opera. Mon-Thu 2400-late, Fri-Sun 2400-late.  Map 4, C6, p252*  This converted theatre became one of the biggest clubs of the *Movida* years. The fashion pack have moved on but it's still fun for an over-the-top night out.

**Kathmandu**, C Señores de Luzón 3, **T** 91 634 42 01.  *Metro Sol or Opera.  Thu 2300-0500, Fri-Sat 2300-0600.  Map 6, B1, p256*  Great

★ **The places to see and be seen**

Best

- Alquimia, Paseo del Prado, p159
- Delic, La Latina, p164
- Café Oliver, Gran Vía, p165
- Star's Café, Gran Vía, p166
- Suite, Gran Vía, p161

funk, friendly crowd and cool DJs at this groovy, red-painted subterranean bar and club.

**Palacio Gaviria**, C Arenal 9, **T** 91 526 60 69/70/71. *Metro Opera. 2230-late, from 2030 on Sun. Map 4, C5, p252* A stunning palace with several high-ceilinged salons, dripping in frescoes and cherubs, each devoted to different music. Dance music and go-go dancers at weekends, but each week night has a different speciality; Wednesday night is tango.

## La Latina and Lavapiés

### Bars

**Bar Baridad**, Costanillo de San Pedro 7, **T** 91 364 18 82. *Metro La Latina. Tue-Sun 1200-2400. Map 2, G2, p248* Tiny, delightfully quirky café-bar with lamps made from buckets and a skeleton under the floor.

**El Bonano**, Plaza Humilladero 4. *Metro La Latina. 1300-1600 and 2000-0100. Map 4, G3, p252* There's always a trendy, young crowd propping up this relaxed little bar overlooking the wide square. Bright modern art hangs on the walls, some basic snacks are served to a mellow soundtrack.

**Champagnería María Pandora**, Plaza Gabriel Miró 1, **T** 91 366 23 70. *Metro La Latina. 1330-1700 and 2100-0200. Map 4, F1, p252* Marble-topped tables, candles, sofas and a crammed bookcase make this a charming and romantic spot. Plus, there's *cava* by the glass and beautiful views from Las Vistillas just a step away

**Delic**, Costanilla de San Andrés (Plaza de Paja) 14, **T** 91 364 54 50. *Metro La Latina. Sun, Tue-Wed 2300-2400, Thu-Sat 1100-2300. Map 4, G2, p252* This retro-looking spot is a relaxing café by day (see p164) and a busy stylish bar by night.

**La Falsa Molestia**, C Magdalena 32, **T** 91 420 32 38, www.lafalsa molestia.com *Metro Antón Martín. Wed-Sun 1200-0200. Map 4, G8, p253* Quirky, ultra-stylish bar and restaurant, with extremely charming staff and mellow music. See also p164.

**La Huerta**, C Lavapiés 9, **T** 91 530 22 81. *Metro Lavapiés or Antón Martín. Tue-Sun 2100-0200. Map 4, G7, p253* Relaxed bar with ceiling frescoes, excellent cocktails and an arty, hippy-ish crowd. Good place to start the night.

**La Peluquería**, C Ave María 44. *Metro Lavapiés. 1200-0300. Map 4, G9, p253* Look out for the old, tiled entrance to this former hairdressers' (hence the name). Inside is a laid-back, cosy bar where you can sip mint tea or a cocktail, or pick up a rug or piece of jewellery; most of what you see is for sale.

**La Ventura**, C Olmo 31, **T** 91 468 04 54. *Metro Antón Martín. Tue-Sat 2200-0500. Map 4, G9, p253* You'd never think it from the outside, but this is one of the best places to hear Madrid's top DJs spinning drum'n'bass, electronica and trip hop. The word is out and it's always packed with a mixed international crowd.

### Clubs

**Danzoo (at Maximes)**, Puerta de Toledo 1. *Metro Puerta deToledo. Fri and Sat 2400-0630. Map 2, H2, p248* Hugely popular, featuring mainly electronica sounds, friendly up-for-it crowd, plenty of room.

# Gran Vía, Malasaña and Chueca

### Bars

**Bluefish**, C San Andrés 26, **T**T91 448 67 65. *Metro Bilbao. Tue-Sun 1300-1600 and 2000-0100. Map 5, E1, p254* This stylish café is also a great place for cocktails; see p165.

**Byron Café**, C San Andrés 32, **T** 615 860 906. *Metro Bilbao. 1630-0330, Fri and Sat until 0430. Closed Sun. Map 5, H2, p254* Wildly psychedelic murals are the backdrop for coffees and cocktails. At night, the mellow music cranks up a gear.

**Café Antik**, C Hortaleza 4, **T** 91 522 21 43. *Metro Gran Vía. Tue-Sun 1700-0200. Map 4, A8, p253* This flamboyant, quirkily decorated cocktail bar is painted in eye-popping colours and specializes in Caribbean cocktails like caipirinhas and mojítos.

**Café del Mercado**, C Fuencarral 43. *Metro Tribunal. Thu-Sat 2200-0300. Map 5, H2, p254* Young trendies pack out this industrial-style bar in the basement of the hip Mercado de Fuencarral shopping complex (see p190). Great sofas for lounging.

**Café Oliver**, C Almirante 12, **T** 91 521 73 79. *Metro Banco de España. Tue-Sat 2100-0300. Map 5, H7, p255* Upstairs is a chic French bistro (unmissable weekend brunches), downstairs is the lounge bar, full of beautiful people sipping expertly mixed cocktails.

**El Café de la Palma**, C Palma 62, **T** 91 522 50 31, www.cafedela palma.net *Metro Noviciado. 1800-0200. Map 2, C3, p248* Excellent chill-out area at the back, comfortable booths in the main area and regular live gigs. Café and bar.

**Chicote**, Gran Vía 12, **T** 91 532 67 37, www.tripfamily.com *Metro Gran Vía. Mon-Thu 2100-0300, Fri-Sat until 0400. Map 4, B9, p253* The grandaddy of all Madrileño cocktail bars, famously a favourite with Ava Gardner and Frank Sinatra. Chicote has preserved its stunning art deco decor and its impossibly glamorous air. Lounge music after midnight.

**Cock**, C Reina 16, **T** 91 532 28 26. *Metro Gran Vía. 1900-0300, Fri-Sat until 0330. Map 4, A9, p253* Established by a bartender trained at *Chicote* (see above), *Cock* is equally glamorous and chi chi. Order the speciality of the house, the exquisite gin fizz.

**La Coctelería**, C Minas 1. *Metro Noviciado. Tue-Sun 2100-0200. Map 2, D3, p248* Thrift-store chic, excellent cocktails and a mellow, loungey soundtrack at this stylish hang-out.

**La Ida**, C Colón 11, **T** 91 522 91 07. *Metro Tribunal. 1200-late. Map 5, G2, p254* Relaxed, arty little café-bar which serves fantastic tea and cakes by day (don't miss the banana and chocolate cake) and gets packed out evenings and weekends.

**Star's Café**, C Marqués de Valdeiglesias 5, **T** 91 522 27 12. *Metro Chueca. Closed Sun. Mon-Fri 0900-2400, Sat-Sun 1200-0130. Map 4, B10, p253* Glitzy, gay-friendly and *muy* fashionable bar-café-restaurant with live music in the week and guest DJs at weekends.

**Stromboli**, C Hortaleza 96. *Metro Chueca. 1600-0300, Thu-Sat until 0330. Map 5, F4, p254* Tongue-in-cheek kitsch with multicoloured 60s-style furniture and excellent chill-out music.

## Clubs

**Barnon**, C Santa Engracia 17, **T** 91 447 38 87. *Metro Alonso Martínez.  2300-0600.  Map 5, C5, p254*  Smart bar and club with retro nights on Tuesdays, funk on Wednesdays and dance music at weekends. Plenty of suits and expensive drinks.

**Coppelia**, Plaza Mostenses 11 (corner of Gran Vía 68), www.coppelia-madrid.com  *Fri-Sat only 0030-0600.  Map 2, D3, p248*  Buzzing club playing deep house and techno on the main dance floor, with trancier sounds in a smaller room. Excellent resident DJs who know how to work the crowd.

**Ministry of Sound at Macumba**, Plaza Estación de Chamartín. *Metro Chamartín.  Map 2, A4, p248*  Once a month, Thursday 2400 until Friday 0600. The Ministry of Sound's glamorous monthly party has become a massive hit on the Madrileño dance scene.

**The Room at Stella**, C Arlabán 7, **T** 91 532 78 33. *Metro Noviciado and Plaza de España.  Fri-Sat only 0100-0600.  Map 4, C9, p253*  This massively popular club night is held in *Stella*, one of the big stars of the *Movida*, which has just been dramatically refurbished. One of the best nights out in the city.

# Salamanca and Paseo Castellana

## Bars

**Déjate Besar**, C Hermanos Bácquer 10, **T** 91 562 54 85. *Metro Núñez de Balboa.  2200-0300, until 0530 Fri-Sat. Closed Sun, Sun-Wed in Aug.  Map 2, A8, p249*  Flashy decor with leopard-skin sofas, movie star paraphernalia and excellent music, attracting a mixed crowd.

**Teatriz**, C Hermosilla 15, **T** 91 577 53 79. *Metro Serrano.*
*1330-1600 and 2030-2330, until 0300 on Fri and Sat. Map 5, E10,*
*p255* Designer bar-restaurant of Philip Starck and Mariscal set in a
converted theatre. One of the best-known in the city; see also
p152.

**Vanitas Vanitatis**, C Velázquez 128, **T** 91 562 65 43. *Metro Núñez*
*de Balboa. 2030-0200, Fri and Sat 2200-0500. Map 2, A9, p249* This
swish, upmarket bar doubles as a club and has a strict door policy.
Great summer terrace.

---

## Clubs

**Fortuny**, C Fortuny 34, **T** 91 319 0588. *Metro Rubén Darío. Mon-Fri*
*1400-0400, Sat-Sun 2100-0400. Map 2, A7, p249* Popular summer
*terraza*, with a dressy, upmarket crowd and the odd celebrity
sighting. Cheerful Euro-pop and Spanish chart music.

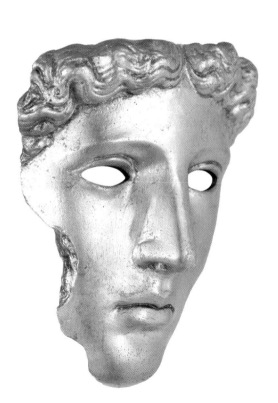

Spain's national theatre and orchestra are based in Madrid, and classical concerts are often held in many small, but delightful, venues like the Fundación Juan March. A night at the opera or the ballet at the opulent Teatro Real is unforgettable and surprisingly affordable. Don't miss the classic home-grown operetta called *zarzuela*; try to see an outdoor performance if you can, held at the Corralla or the Jardines de Sabatini. Otherwise the Teatro de la Zarzuela has a year-round programme. There are bars and clubs catering to all other kinds of live music, particularly jazz and blues. Madrid is also, perhaps surprisingly, one of the best places to see flamenco in Spain. Besides the *tablaos*, the theatres often feature some of the best-known dance troupes and singers, so it's always worth having a look at the listings magazines mentioned below. And if you just want a quiet night at the movies, head for the delightful art deco Cine Doré. Ticket prices vary according to performances, but are usually considerably less than London or New York prices.

The weekly guide *La Guía del Ocio*, www.guiadelocio.com, in Spanish only, is available from kiosks and has extensive theatre, music and opera listings. It's pretty good for live music too, but rubbish when it comes to clubs and bars. For what's going on in Madrid's ever-changing nightlife, get flyers from the Mercado del Fuencarral (see below) or pick up a copy of the English-language monthly newspaper *InMadrid*, with reviews of the latest bars and clubs. The free *What's On* guide from the tourist office has some cultural listings in English. On Fridays, the daily newspapers *El Mundo* and *ABC* both produce entertainment supplements which can be useful, and you can pick up the freebie *LaNetro*, www.madrid.netro.com, in most shops (all in Spanish). Also see www.madridhoy.net

## Cinema

Spanish cinema is enjoying a high profile outside Spain, thanks to the success of people like Penélope Cruz (from Madrid); the director who made her famous, Pedro Almodóvar; and Alejandro Amenábar, who directed *The Others* with Nicole Kidman and the excellent *Abre los Ojos* (remade as the dire *Vanilla Sky*). Less well known but equally respected Spanish directors to look out for include David Trevor; the experimental film-maker Julio Medem; Alex de la Iglesia, whose film *El Día de la Bestia* has become a cult favourite; and Bigas Luna, whose films are almost fetishistic in their devotion to detail. Cinema-going is very popular in Madrid, and, while there are dozens of cinemas showing dubbed versions of the latest Hollywood schlock, there are plenty of smaller art house cinemas which show a more offbeat selection of foreign or experimental films. The cinema is cheap by most European standards, and is cheaper still on the *día del espectador*, which is usually Monday or Wednesday. Screenings around 2200 to 2300 sell the quickest, so you stand a better chance of getting tickets for the most popular films if you don't mind an earlier showing.

**Cine Estudio del Círculo de Bellas Artes**, C Marqués de Casa Riera 2, **T** 91 522 50 92. *Metro Banco de España.  Map 4, C11, p253* Arthouse cinema attached to the Círculo de Bellas Artes (see p77).

**Cinesa Capitol**, Gran Vía 41, **T** 902 33 32 31. *Metro Callao.  Map 4, A5, p252* One of several beautiful, old cinemas from the early 20th century. There are great hand-painted billboards advertising its programme but films are almost always dubbed.

**Filmoteca Nacional**, Cine Doré, C Santa Isabel 3, **T** 91 549 00 11. *Metro Antón Martín.  Ticket office open 1600-2245, bookshop open 1700-2230, bar-restaurant 1600-2400 (**T** 91 369 49 23).  Map 4, G9, p253* The home of the National Film Institute, this endearing art deco cinema puts on a varied programme of classics, foreign language films and film festivals. Outdoor screenings on the roof terrace in summer.

**Ideal Yelmo Cineplex**, C Doctor Cortezo 6, **T** 91 369 25 18. *Metro Sol or Tirso de Molina.  Map 6, E8, p256* Huge multiplex which shows most of the Hollywood blockbusters with Spanish subtitles. Monday is cheaper.

**Pequeño Cine Estudio**, C Magallanes 1, **T** 91 531 63 61. *Metro Quevedo.  Map 2, A4, p248* Delightful little art house cinema which mainly shows the classics from Hollywood's Golden Age.

## Dance

As a major European capital, Madrid hosts the finest dance companies from around the world and you might also get a chance to see the Madrid-based Ballet Nacional de España (Spanish National Ballet), or the more contemporary Compañía Nacional de Danza. Look out too for Victor Ullate's Ballet de la Comunidad de Madrid, an experimental mix of classical and contemporary ballet. Barcelona is better known for its experimental dance, but there is usually plenty going on in Madrid if you dig through the listings magazines mentioned above and the Sala Cuarta Pared (see below) often hosts interesting contemporary dance. The annual Madrid en Danza festival (see p184) is a good chance to check out up-and-coming dance groups. Madrid's flamenco scene is as vibrant as anywhere in Spain; there are dozens of places to hear and see flamenco in all its styles, from the most traditional to the latest trends, inspired by dancers like Joaquín Cortés or Joaquín Grilo, and music groups like Ketama who have added a contemporary twist to the traditional movements and music.

**Centro Cultural de la Villa**, Plaza de Colón s/n, **T** 91 575 60 80. *Metro Colón. Map 5, F9, p255* Madrid's main municipal arts centre, with an interesting programme of dance, music and drama. It regularly hosts zarzuela during the summer (see box, p178), and is one of the main venues for Madrid en Danza, the annual dance festival, see p184.

**Sala Cuarta Pared**, C Ercilla 7, Arganzuela, **T** 91 517 23 17. *Metro Embajadores.* This is one of the best venues in Madrid for contemporary dance and is also a good place to find experimental drama productions.

**Teatro de Madrid**, Av de la Ilustración, **T** 91 740 53 72. *Metro Barrio del Pilar.* This new theatre in the northwest of the city hosts contemporary drama and dance performances.

**Teatro Real**, Plaza de Isabel II, **T** 91 516 06 60. *Metro Opera. Map 4, C3, p252* Madrid's beautifully restored opera house (see p65) provides an opulent venue for opera and ballet.

## Flamenco

**Café de Chinitas**, C Torrija 7, **T** 91 559 51 35. *Metro Santo Domingo. Closed Sun. Map 4, A3, p252* Dinner and a flamenco performance at one of the oldest flamenco venues (*tablaos*) in the city. The performers are well known for their excellence, but it's very touristy and expensive. Book well in advance.

**Candela**, C Olmo 2, **T** 91 467 33 82. *Metro Antón Martín. Map 4, G8, p253* A celebrated flamenco bar which hosts occasional performances and is very popular with flamenco artists and those who come to gawp at them. The atmosphere gets better later on.

**Larios Café**, C Silva, 4, **T** 91 547 93 94. *Metro Santo Domingo or Callao. 2100-0400. Map 4, A5, p252* Gorgeous, award-winning art deco-esque interior; Cuban food in the restaurant and salsa, flamenco and funk on the dance floor. Restaurant-bar-club venue.

**Las Carboneras**, Plaza del Conde de Miranda 1, **T** 91 542 86 77. *Metro Sol. Map 6, C2, p256* Flamenco *tablao*, which has breath-takingly skilful dancers, musicians and singers, but is slightly lacking in atmosphere.

**Casa Patas**, C Cañizares 10, **T** 91 369 04 96. *Metro Antón Martín. Map 4, F8, p253* The stage is in a shadowy, intimate little room at the back of the bar-restaurant area; it's small enough to feel the sweat of the performers as they whirl about the stage, and you can't help joining in with the odd 'olé'. The flamenco performances are among the best in the city.

**Peña Chaquetón**, C Canarias 39, **T** 91 671 27 77. *Metro Palos de la Frontera.* Performances on Friday nights only, but get there early or you won't have a hope of getting in. It may be basic, but

**Fan flirtations**
*Madrileños coquettishly dance the dance for onlookers outside the Museo del Prado.*

this is generally considered to be one of the very best flamenco venues in the city.

**La Soleá**, Cava Baja 27, **T** 91 365 33 08. *Metro La Latina. Map 4, G3, p252* Anything can happen at this famous flamenco bar where guitarists and singers gather for semi-impromptu performances. You won't be alone as the bar is propped up mostly by *guiris* (young foreigners) nowadays, yet it still retains a magical atmosphere.

## Music

You'd almost expect the former capital of Spain's colonial empire to boast a pulsating Latin music scene. It does – and then some. This is a great city for hip-wiggling to live salsa and merengue bands well beyond the wee, small hours, or getting passionate about some real Argentine tango. The capital also looks south across the Mediterranean for musical inspiration and there's always a good selection of African musicians to enjoy on any night of the week. For a national flavour, there are flamenco clubs where you can hear the authentic sounds of the south. Neither is the city syncopatedly challenged, with enough smoky, subterranean jazz and blues venues to satisfy even the most discerning of cats. The local rock and pop scene is vibrant and Madrid pulls in its fair share of stadium rockers (U2 and their ilk) at its large, custom-built arenas.

Madrid's status as capital city ensures it is an obvious stopping point for the biggest names in classical and contemporary music from around Europe. Spain's national choir and orchestra are based at the Auditorio Nacional and the Teatro Real is presently home to the Orquesta Sinfónica de Madrid. The Teatro Real also hosts opera, performed by international and Spanish companies. As far as contemporary music goes, there's something to suit everyone, from regular appearances by the teenagers' favourite crooner, David Bisbal (winner of the 2002 reality TV show, *Operación*

*Triunfo*), to smoky underground blues bars, as well as big riverside venues where you can catch the biggest international bands.

## Contemporary (rock, pop, jazz, roots, folk, country, world)

**Berlin Cabaret**, C Costanillo de San Pedro 11, **T** 91 366 20 34. *Metro La Latina.* *Map 6, F1, p256*  A deliberate throw-back to the 1930s, this classic bar has two floors, and puts on an eccentric variety of shows; besides the regular, slightly saucy cabaret acts, you might also find magic acts or stand-up comics.

**Café Central**, Plaza del Angel 10, **T** 91 369 41 43.  *Metro Sol.* *Map 4, E8, p253*  One of Madrid's loveliest jazz venues, set in an elegant, art deco café with huge burnished mirrors. Local and international groups play at the evening sessions, but even if you don't catch a live show, it's the perfect place to while away an afternoon with a coffee, newspaper and some soft jazz in the background.

**Café Libertad 8**, C Libertad 8, **T** 91 532 1150.  *Metro Chueca.* *Map 4, A10, p253*  Several of Spain's best-known musicians apparently got their start in this relaxed café-bar, which regularly features up-and-coming bands.

**Café del Mercado**, Puerta de Toledo s/n, **T** 91 365 87 39.  *Metro Puerta de Toledo.* *Map 2, H2, p248*  Despite being tucked away in the ill-starred Mercado de Toledo development (see p74), this is a popular salsa bar and club with regular live gigs.

**La Coquette**, C Hileras 14.  *Metro Opera.* *Map 4, C4, p252*  Tiny underground blues bar which fulfills every cliché in the book: smoky, louche, and loud. Fabulous. Live blues Tuesday to Thursday.

## ▶ Zarzuela

Zarzuela is Madrid's very own light operetta. It got its name from the **Palacio de la Zarzuela** on the outskirts of Madrid where the earliest performances were created for the entertainment of Felipe IV and his court. The stories were usually sugary and sentimental, sometimes spiced up with a little contemporary gossip based on local events – one even describes the grand opening of the Gran Vía. They were hugely popular right up until the Civil War but only just made it through the repressive years of Franco's dictatorship. Still, zarzuela has been enjoying a bit of a revival over the past couple of decades; in summer, try and catch an outdoor performance at **La Corrala** (see p75), or at the **Jardines de Sabatini** (see p65). The delightful **Teatro de la Zarzuela** (Calle Jovellanes 4, **T** 91 524 54 00. Metro Banco de España) holds performances all year.

**Populart**, C Huertas 22, **T** 91 429 8407. *Metro Antón Martín. Map 4, F10, p253* Hugely popular, lively club featuring live jazz and blues, with occasional appearances by Latin and world music bands. It's got a great reputation and pulls in some well-known groups, but it's best during the week; weekends can get too crammed.

**La Riviera**, Paseo Bajo Virgen del Puerto s/n, Puente de Segovia, **T** 91 365 24 15. *Metro Puerta del Angel.* Beautiful art deco-style concert venue near the river with a retractable roof. Mainly rock, indie and pop acts on the programme, but it has hosted some big international names. It doubles as a club, too.

**Sala Clamores**, C Albuquerque 14, **T** 91 445 79 38. *Metro Bilbao. Map 5, B3, p254* Popular jazz and world music venue.

**Siroco**, C San Dimas 3, **T** 91 593 30 70. *Metro Noviciado*. *Map 2, C3, p248* All kinds of home-grown rock, indie and alternative bands show up on the programme of this laid-back music venue, which also doubles up as an excellent little club.

**Suristán**, C Cruz 7, **T** 91 532 39 09. *Metro Sevilla*. *Map 4, D8, p253* This is a great place to catch all kinds of world music, from Latin rhythms to African jazz. It attracts a more diverse crowd than many of Madrid's nightspots, especially at weekends. When the bands are finished DJs keep the party going until late.

## Classical and opera

**Auditorio Nacional de Música**, C Príncipe de Vergara, **T** 91 337 01 00. *Metro Cruz de Rayo or Prosperidad*. Home of Spain's national choir and orchestra and Madrid's main venue for classical music. Tickets available at the box office or through *Caja Madrid*, **T** 902 488 488.

**Fundación Juan March**, C Castelló 77, **T** 91 435 42 40. *Metro Núñez de Balboa*. *Map 2, B9, p249* This elegant exhibition space hosts regular chamber concerts and recitals, including lunchtime concerts which are usually free.

**Teatro Real**, Plaza de Isabel II, **T** 91 516 06 60. *Metro Opera*. *Map 4, C3, p252* Madrid's beautifully restored opera house (see p65) provides an opulent venue for opera and ballet.

# Theatre

Madrid's theatrical tradition stretches back to the Golden Age of Lope de Vega, Calderón de la Barca and Tirso de Molina, and the city is strewn with dozens of venues featuring all kinds of work from the traditional renditions of the classics to avant-garde contemporary performances. The most prominent classical theatre companies, Centro Dramático Nacional and the Compañía Nacional de Teatro Clásico, are based at the Teatro María Guerrero and the Teatro de la Comedia respectively. For the most interesting contemporary performances, check what's on at the Sala Cuarta Pared (see p173), the Mirador or the Círculo de Bellas Artes.

**Círculo de Bellas Artes**, C Marqués de Casa Riera 2, **T** 91 532 44 37 (information), **T** 902 42 24 42 (tickets). *Metro Banco de España. Map 4, C11, p253* This art deco exhibition space and café (see p77) hosts innovative performances regularly.

**Teatro Calderón**, C Atocha 18, **T** 91 429 58 90. *Metro Tirso de Molina.* Everything from musicals to opera, modern dance to classical drama.

**Teatro de la Comedia**, C Príncipe 14, **T** 91 521 49 31. *Metro Sol. Map 4, D9, p253* Another grand theatre hosting classical performances. Home to the Compañía Nacional de Teatro Clásico.

**Teatro Español**, C Príncipe 25, **T** 91 429 62 97. *Metro Sol.* (Closed for restoration at the time of writing; call for more information.) *Map 4, D9, p253* Classical Spanish drama.

**Teatro María Guerrero**, C Tamayo y Baus 4, **T** 91 319 4769, **T** 902 488 488. *Metro Colón or Chueca. Map 5, H7, p255* Just west of the Paseo de Recoletos, this beautiful old theatre is home to the Centro Dramático Nacional.

Madrileños love a party and festivals provide an excellent excuse. The city's biggest festival is the Fiesta de San Isidro (see p184), a two-week long party which erupts in the streets with traditional music and dancing. The local dance is called the *chotis* and you'll see it danced by women in flouncy dresses with carnations tucked in their hair and men in caps and checked coats. There are plenty of other traditional festivals, some of which are still in touch with their religious roots, like the pilgrimage from La Paloma in La Latina (see p185). You can also catch some bizarre traditional ceremonies, like the Burial of the Sardine (see p183) that marks the end of winter. There are excellent cultural festivals, from the spring dance festival, Madrid en Danza, to the Festival de Otoño (see p186), devoted to the performing arts. Festimad is a huge music festival held in a Madrildeño suburb. Check details of festivals in advance; for more information, see the cultural agenda section of the city's website, www.munimadrid.es, contact tourist offices (see p30) or the T010 city information line.

## January

**Noche Vieja** (New Year), sees everyone flocking to the Puerta del Sol for midnight where it's traditional to eat a grape for luck at each chime of the clock.

**Cabalgata de los Reyes** (5 January) is held in towns throughout Spain. The Three Kings, or *Los Reyes*, parade in floats, the *cabalgata*, tossing out sweets and presents to children. Children get their Christmas presents the following day, the *Día de los Reyes*.

## February

**Carnival** is held in the week before Lent and is a good excuse for a party with dressing-up, floats, parades and street parties. The festivities finish up with the bizarre ritual of the Entierro de la Sardina, or Burial of the Sardine, which marks the end of winter and the beginning of spring.

**La Alternativa** is an alternative theatre and dance festival is held some time in February or March at venues throughout the city. Check with the tourist office for exact dates.

**ARCO** is a massive, month-long contemporary art fair held in the Parque Ferial Juan Carlos I near the airport. For more information, **T** 91 722 50 00, www.arco.ifema.es

## March/April

**Semana Santa** (Holy Week) is celebrated with solemn processions and masses in Toledo and, to a lesser extent, in Madrid. It's not such a big event as in southern Spain, but you'll still see some processions of venerated statues surrounded by members of different confraternities in their strange pointed hoods. The most startling is the procession of the brotherhood of Jesús Nazareno el Pobre which parades around the neighbourhood of La Latina. On 23 April the King and Queen present the prestigious literary prize, the **Premio Cervantes de Literatura**, at Alcalá University.

## May

**Fiesta Dos de Mayo** Celebrated in Madrid on 2 May which is the anniversary of its uprising against the Napoleonic forces. It features live bands in the Plaza Dos de Mayo and various events in the theatres and cultural venues.

**Corpus Christi** in Toledo consists of religious celebrations and processions, held eight weeks after Easter.

**Festimad** (mid-late May) is a massive outdoor music festival held in the suburb of Mostoles.

**Fiestas de San Isidro** (second week of May) The fiesta is devoted to Madrid's patron saint and has developed into a massive event with live bands, parades and street parties all over the city. It also marks the opening of the bullfighting season with several special bullfighting events.

**Madrid en Danza** (Mid-May to mid-June) An International Dance Festival held in venues all over the city. It's a great opportunity to see everything from new contemporary dance, to flamenco or ballet.

## June

**Fiesta de San Antonio de la Florida** (13 June) is celebrated with a big street party near the hermitage of San Antonio de la Florida, which is decorated with Goya's frescoes.

**PhotoEspaña** (Mid-June to mid-July) is an international photography festival with exhibitions, workshops and talks. For more information, **T** 91 360 13 20, www.photoes.ya.com

**Día de San Juan** (24 June) is a midsummer festival which is not such big news in Madrid as it is elsewhere in Spain, but there are fireworks and musicians in the Parque del Buen Retiro.

## July

**The Festival del Verano** (17-25 July) is the Summer Festival held in Avila with street parties, parades, bullfights and live music. A similar festival is held over several weeks in Segovia during July and August.

**Veranos de la Villa** (from July to September). Summers in the City is the largest city-sponsored arts festival in Madrid, with a range of activities spanning theatre, dance and music.

## August

**Motín de Aranjuez** (during the first week of August) is a huge fiesta held in Aranjuez recalling the historic mutiny which took place in 1808. Many people dress up in period costumes.

**Verbenas de San Cayetano**, **San Lorenzo** and **La Paloma** (6-15 August) are colourful, traditional street festivals held in the old neighbourhoods of La Latina and Lavapiés.

**Fiesta de San Lorenzo** (10 August) held at El Escorial is a celebration of El Escorial's patron saint's day with parades and a huge fair.

## September-November

**Festival de Otoño** (Autumn Festival), focuses on the performing arts and runs from late September until November. It features theatre, dance and music performances, complementary exhibitions, plus a vigorous programme of talks and other events.

**Feria de Aranjuez** (first week of September) is the re-enactment of a famous local mutiny and other festivities.

**Festival de Jazz de Madrid** is an international jazz festival that draws some big names and is very enjoyable. It usually runs throughout October.

**Fiesta de Santa Teresa** (15 October) in Avila with enormously popular processions and festivities for Saint Teresa.

**Fiesta de San Frutas** (25 October) has celebrations for Segovia's patron saint.

**Fiesta de la Virgen de la Almudena** (9 November) is celebrated with a Mass held in the Plaza Mayor for the city's female patron saint (see box, p67).

## December

**Feria de Artesanía**  Shops fill with traditional decorations for crib scenes and there's a huge craft market held in the Recoletos.

Shopping

As Spain's capital, Madrid contains every kind of shop imaginable, from excellent fresh food markets like the lovely Mercado de San Miguel (see p192), to tiny, old-fashioned shops which haven't changed in decades, to grand glitzy shopping malls where you can get everything you want under one roof. It's also kitsch-lovers' heaven with a dazzling array of fabulous tack. As a general guide, you can find almost anything you want in the streets around Calle Preciados in the centre: department stores, chain stores, individual shops selling everything from hams to traditional Madrileño cloaks. The northwestern neighbourhoods of Argüelles and Moncloa, particularly Calle Princesa, are also good for department stores and fashion chains.

The kiosks on Puerta del Sol have international newspapers. Smart Salamanca has plenty of designer fashion boutiques and interior decoration shops at prices to make you gasp. Chueca is full of hip, unusual fashion and music shops as well as the shoe-shoppers' heaven along Calle Augusto Figueroa.

Most shops open around 1000 until 1300 and then reopen about 1600 until 2000 or 2100. Large chain stores, department stores and shopping malls usually stay open all day and some don't close until 2200. Some smaller shops will only open Saturday morning, while almost all shops, including supermarkets, are closed on Sundays – worth remembering if you are only here for the weekend.

## Books and newspapers

**La Casa de Libro**, Gran Vía 29. *Metro Gran Vía. Map 4, A7, p253* Enormous, central bookshop with a fairly small selection of English titles.

**Fnac**, C Preciados 28. *Metro Sol or Callao. Map 4, B6, p252* Massive store packed with books, DVDs, CDs, videos and electronic goods. There's also a travel agency, a newspaper shop (with very little in English) and a concert ticket agency.

**Librería Altaïr**, C Gastambide 31. *Metro Argüelles. Map 2, B2, p248* Excellent travel bookshop, with maps, magazines and an exhaustive range of guides.

## Department stores and shopping malls

**ABC Serrano Centro Comercial**, C Serrano 61. *Metro Serrano. Map 5, B10, p255* Shopping centre housed in the former ABC newspaper building. It has the usual array of fast-food outlets and chain stores plus a smattering of upmarket shops selling household goods and fashion.

**El Corte Inglés**, C Preciados 2-3. *Metro Sol. Map 4, C6, p252* One of several branches of Spain's biggest department store: including a basement supermarket and gourmet shop. Other services include a cafeteria, bureau de change, travel agency and ticket outlet.

There are two stores devoted to books and music respectively at the corner of Calle Preciados and the Puerta del Sol.

## Fashion and accessories

**Camper**, C Preciados 75. *Metro Argüelles*. *Map 4, B6, p252* There are branches of this hugely popular shoe store all over the city. Bright, comfortable and playful, this footwear is also much cheaper than outside Spain.

**Farrutx**, C Serrano 7. *Metro Serrano*. *Map 5, H9, p255* Quite simply, shoes to die for.

**Glam**, C Hortaleza 62. *Metro Gran Vía*. *Map 5, H3, p254* Provocative clubwear – plenty of lycra and spangles.

**Loewe**, C Serrano 34. *Metro Serrano*. *Map 5, E10, p255* Luxury leather goods and ultra-fashionable clothes for men and women who don't have to look at price tags. One of several upmarket labels represented on this street and those around it.

**Mango**, C Arenal 24. *Metro Opera*. *Map 4, C5, p252* Another runaway Spanish chain, *Mango* offers the latest women's fashions and accessories in decent fabrics.

**Marmota**, C Río Baja 13. *Metro Puerta de Toledo*. *Map 2, H2, p248* There's a clutch of fabulous vintage clothes stores in this street and around; this one has the best prices.

**Mercado de Fuencarral**, C Fuencarral 45. *Metro Gran Vía*. *Map 5, H2, p254* All kinds of small boutiques on two floors selling alternative clothes, accessories and underwear for young hipsters. Don't miss *Divina Providencia* on the top floor for original dresses and bags. There's a very popular basement bar, too (see p165).

**Mitsuoko**, C Mayor 36. *Metro Sol or Opera. Map 6, A3, p256*
Cool, sexy women's fashion, with a café area.

**Purificación García**, C Serrano 28 and 92. *Metro Serrano. Map 5, E10, p255* A chain of sleek minimalist-style shops, offering equally sleek minimalist-style designs for trendy urban women.

**Tamburi y Hereza**, C Fuencarral 43. *Metro Gran Vía or Tribunal. Map 5, H2, p254* The quirky clothes are great, but it's the super-funky bags and accessories which really stand out here.

**Zara**, C Gran Vía 32. *Metro Callao. Map 4, A7, p253* You are never far from a branch of this fashion chain which is the best bet for stylish clothes, shoes and accessories at really low prices. Real bargain-hunters should head next door to the *Zara* seconds shop.

## Food and drink

**Caramelos Paco**, C Toledo 55. *Metro La Latina. Map 4, G5, p252* Famous old sweet shop selling all kinds of sugary concoctions in lurid colours; worth a visit for the window displays alone. Across the street is *Fiestas Paco* with everything you need for a party, from hats and streamers to paper plates.

**Casa Mira**, C San Jerónimo 30. *Metro Sol. Map 6, A3, p256* Lovely, old-fashioned baker which sells all kinds of goodies, displayed on a revolving glass stand. It's *the* place to buy *turrón*, a delicious honey-flavoured soft nougat, which is traditionally eaten around Christmas.

**La Mallorquina**, Puerta del Sol 2. *Metro Sol. Map 6, A8, p256* Classic old pastry shop on the Puerta del Sol with incredibly low prices.

**Mantequerías González**, C León 12. *Metro Antón Martín. Map 4. E9, p253* Fabulous range of gourmet deli items and you can sample them in the pleasant little bar area at the back. Wine, olive oil, luxurious tins and jars of anchovies and other delicacies, which make good presents, and a great range of cheeses and cured meats. Very friendly staff.

**Mariano Madrueño**, C Postigo San Martín. *Metro Callao. Map 4, B5, p252* Charming, century-old wine sellers with an excellent range of Spanish wines as well as some interesting regional liqueurs.

**El Palacio de los Quesos**, C Mayor 53. *Metro Sol or Opera. Map 6, A3, p256* 'The Palace of Cheeses' contains a dazzling display of cheeses from all over Spain, from the delicate Galician tetilla to classic manchego.

---

### Markets

**Cuesta de Claudio Moyano**. *Metro Atocha. Map 2, H7, p249* Second-hand bookstalls line this pretty street near Atocha station. Most are open daily and the stalls are always good for a rummage.

**Mercado de San Miguel**, Plaza de San Miguel, see p58. *Metro Sol. Closed Sat afternoon and Sun. Map 6, C2, p256* Set in a turn-of-the-century listed building, this is probably Madrid's prettiest market. Dozens of stalls sell all kinds of fresh produce from fish to cheese, as well as a fantastic array of cured meats.

**Mercado de Sellos y Monedas**. *Metro Sol. Map 6, C4, p256* This stamp and coin market is held in Plaza Mayor on Sunday mornings.

**El Rastro** Madrid's legendary Sunday morning flea market, see p74.

> ### Heavenly sweets

The cloistered nuns have had to find new ways to fund their communities in Spain's new democratic era. Some have reverted to the old practice of making delicious cakes, sweets and jams. They are usually open at lunchtime and late afternoon.

**Convento de las Carboneras**, C Codo. Metro La Latina or Sol. This is a little hard to find, tucked down a small passageway just off the Plaza del Villa. Press the buzzer marked 'monjas' (nuns) and you will ushered down a corridor and given a list of *dulces*, or cakes, to choose from. The money is put into a revolving drum and your cakes and change will come out the other side.

**Monasterio de la Visitación**, C San Bernardo 72. Metro San Bernardo. All kinds of cakes and marmalades, but their speciality is the *pasta de Santa Eulalia*, a scrumptious pastry.

---

### Souvenirs and unusual shops

**La Tienda de Real Madrid**, Centro Comercial La Esquina del Bernabeu, C Concha Espina 1. *Metro Santiago Bernabeu.* A mecca for football fans: strips, scarves, caps and other memorabilia emblazoned with Real Madrid's logo.

**Casa Seseña**, C Cruz 23. *Metro Sol. Map 4, D8, p253* This delightful old shop is the only place left in Madrid which still makes the traditional Madrileño cloaks. Current window displays show photographs of Hilary Clinton wearing her Seseña cloak.

**Maty**, C Maestro Victoria 2. *Metro Opera*. *Map 4, C6, p252* Packed with flouncy flamenco dresses, shoes, hair combs, casta- nets and other accessories. The tiny dresses for girls are adorable.

**El Flamenco Vive**, C Conde de Lemos 7. *Metro Opera*. *Map 4, D3, p252* Specialist flamenco shop with a fantastic range of books and CDs. This is also the place to come to find out what's really going on in the flamenco scene, with lots of flyers and posters.

**Manuel González Contreras**, C Mayor 80. *Metro Sol*. *Map 4, E2, p252* Beautiful handmade guitars.

**Botería de Julio Rodriíguez**, C Aguila 12. *Metro La Latina*. *Map 4, H3, p252* Handmade traditional *botas de vino* or wineskins. This family have been making them for more than 150 years.

**Belsol**, C Travesía de Belén 3. *Metro Chueca*. *Map 4, G5, p254* Exquisite, handmade and very original lampshades in silk, paper and other fabrics. They can also convert any object you choose into a lamp.

## Sport shops

**Koala**, C León 29, www.koala-deportes *Metro Antón Martín*. *Map 4, F9, 253* Fine selection of sports equipment, specializing in hiking, mountain climbing and skiing.

**Calmera**, C Atocha 98. *Metro Antón Martín*. *Map 4, H11, p253* Huge bike shop with a wide range of bikes, equipment, maps and guides. Also has info on bike tours in the surrounding sierras.

**Stance**, C Duque de Sevilla 16. *Metro Cruz del Rayo*. Everything you need for skateboarding or snowboarding.

Among the top-selling daily newspapers in Madrid are two that are devoted exclusively to football, *La Marca* and *AS*. Walk along any street on the night of a big Real Madrid or Atlético de Madrid match and you'll see everyone in every bar glued to the TV. Football, as the cliché goes, is a Spanish religion, closely followed by basketball. Getting tickets to either is difficult but not impossible. The city's sports facilities have improved dramatically over the last decade, and there are several municipally run sports centres with pools and gyms that offer a good range of other sports. For general information on municipal sports facilities, call T 91 540 39 39. The Parque del Buen Retiro and the Casa de Campo are good for cycling, jogging, and strolling, but you should head out to the mountains for some serious hiking, mountain climbing and biking. There are even a couple of ski stations less than an hour's drive from the city, but these are best avoided at weekends when they get very crowded.

## Adventure sports

**Arawak Viajes**, C Peñuelas12, **T** 91 474 25 24, **F** 91 474 52 76, www.geocities.com/arawak_viajes  *Metro Embajadores*.  Activities include hiking in the sierras, skiing, diving, mountain climbing, plus other activities including speleology, rafting, horse riding, canyon descent, hang-gliding, quad biking.

**Adrenalin Sport**, C Serrano 141, **T** 91 411 7564, www.tst.es/atodoplan  *Metro Gregorio Marañón*.  If you want to do some bungee-jumping this is the place to come.

**Hacienda Huella**, C José Abascal 32, **T** 91 593 04 41, www.haciendohuella.com  *Metro Iglesia*.  Walking tours in the sierras around Madrid.

## Basketball

Madrid has two major basketball teams: Adecco Estudiantes, wwww.clubestudiantes.com and Real Madrid, www.realmadrid.es Matches were held in the huge Palacio de Deportes that burned down in 2001 and is now being rebuilt. In the meantime, most matches take place in the Palacio Vistalegre, Av Plaza de Toros s/n, Carabanchel, T 91 422 07 80, www.palaciovistalegre.com/

## Bullfighting

**Plaza de Toros Monumental de las Ventas**, C Alcalá 237, **T** 91 356 22 00, www.las-ventas.com  *Metro Ventas*.  The bullfighting season runs between April and September; tickets are cheaper when booked at the bullring rather than through an agency. See also p92.

## Cycling and mountain biking

**Esto es Madrid**, C Torpedero Tucumán 18, **T** 91 350 11 60, www.estoesmadrid.net *Metro Pío XII*. Mountain biking tours in and around Madrid; includes a women-only bike tour. Bike hire prices vary, but you'll probably pay about €4-5 per hour or €15-20 per day. See Directory, p216.

## Football

Football tickets can cost anywhere from €15-60.

**Estadio del Rayo Vallecano**, Arroyo del Olivar 49, **T** 91 478 22 53, www.rayovallecano.es/ *Metro Portazgo*. The home stadium of Madrid's little-known third team.

**Estadio Santiago Bernabeu**, Paseo de la Castellana 104, **T** 91 398 43 00, www.realmadrid.es/ *Metro Santiago Bernabeu*. Real Madrid's stadium.

**Estadio Vicente Calderón**, **T** 91 366 47 07, www.clubatletico demadrid.com/ *Metro Pirámides*. Madrid's second team, Atlético de Madrid, play here.

## Golf

**Club de Campo Villa de Madrid**, Carretera de Castilla Km 2, **T** 91 550 20 10. Eighteen holes, plus tennis courts, pool and restaurant. Members only, so call in advance.

**El Olivar de la Hinojosa**, Av de Dublin, **T** 91 721 18 89. A nine-hole course, an 18-hole course, plus squash, tennis and restaurant. Members only, so call in advance.

## Gyms

**Avanti**, C Isaac Peral 14, **T** 91 544 83 20, www.avanti.
turincon.com  *Metro Moncloa*.  Yoga and t'aichi as well as regular
gym activities.

**Arián**, C Flora 3, **T** 91 559 05 14.  *Metro Opera*.  Aerobic classes,
yoga, martial arts, capoeira and aikido. There's also a tiny pool.

## Jogging

**Los Jardines del Retiro** (p43) are the shadiest and most
attractive area to jog in the city centre.

**La Casa de Campo** (p82) has acres of unspoilt woodland and
is popular for jogging and mountain biking. This park is well
known for prostitutes, but they tend to stay in certain areas close
to the roads.

## Skiing

There are three ski stations close to Madrid. None is particularly
high and the slopes are ideal for beginners or families. Only Puerta
de Navacerrada has accommodation close by.

**Puerta de Navacerrada**. Information in Madrid: C Casado de
Alisal 7, **T** 91 230 55 72. Sixty kilometres north of Madrid with 12
slopes, five chair lifts, six ski lifts and one children's ski lift.

**Valcotos**. Information in Madrid: C Felipe IV 12, **T** 91 239 75 03.
Seventy kilometres north of Madrid, with 10 slopes, two chair lifts
and six ski lifts. Generally considered to be the prettiest resort.

Sports

**Valdesquí**. Information in Madrid: C San Ramón Nonato 1, **T** 91 215 59 39. Seventy three kilometres north of Madrid, with eight slopes, two chair lifts, six ski lifts and two children's ski lifts.

## Swimming and municipal sports centres

The following municipal sports centres all have outdoor pools, gyms, tennis courts and other sports. Entry to pools costs around €4.

**Barrio del Pilar**, Av de Monforte de Lemos, s/n, **T** 91 314 79 43. *Metro Barrio del Pilar or Begoña*. **Casa de Campo**, Av del Angel s/n, **T** 91 463 00 50. *Metro Lago or Puerta del Angel*. **La Elipa**, Prolongación de O'Donnell, s/n, **T** 91 430 35 11. *Metro La Estrella*.

## Walking and climbing

There is some excellent walking in the beautiful sierras that surround Madrid and are, amazingly, less than an hour's drive away. The best bases are Navacerrada and Cercedilla to the north of the city, and there are several good walking guides to the area, including Jaqueline Oglesby's *Mountains of Central Spain* (Cicerone 1996). For guided tours into the mountains, see Adventure Sports above.

## Yoga

**Centro de Yoga Avagar**, C Bravo Murillo 243, 1°, **T** 91 579 72 82. *Metro Tetuan*.

**Yoga Center**, C Lagasca 32, 1°, **T** 91 575 15 42, www.yogacenter.es *Metro Retiro*. Daily classes in Hatha, Iyengar and Ashtanga Vinyasa yoga.

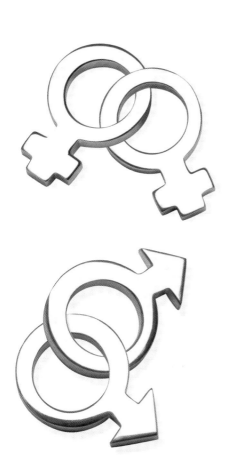

Chueca is the heart of the city's gay scene, packed with shops, restaurants, bars and clubs. Madrid as a whole is not especially gay-friendly (most Madrileños being of the 'out of sight, out of mind' mentality, rather than downright disapproving), but Chueca has become a village unto itself, where nearly every shop and bar displays its rainbow stickers with pride.

Like most major cities, the really fashionable clubs are gay ones attracting a mixed clientele. COGAM runs an excellent helpline for visitors, too. For night-life, get the free *Shanguide*, available in Chueca's bars and cafés, or the ultra-hip fashion freebie, *Shangay*. Others include *Zero* for news and current events, and *Gesto* for up-to-the-minute cultural news. *GO* and *Ciclo* are available all over Spain and are not especially Madrid-orientated. Gay nightlife is *el ambiente* in Spanish and many mainstream listing magazines have a small section under this heading. Useful websites: www.guiagay.com, www.chueca.com and www.corazongay.com, in Spanish. In English: www.gaywired.com and www.gay.com

**COGAM**, C Espíritu Santo 37, **T** 91 522 45 17, **T** 91 523 00 70. This is a collective of gay and lesbian organizations, which encompass several political and social groups. It publishes a magazine, *Entiendes*, which is available at most bookshops and bars in Chueca. It also has an information line (Gay Inform, see below), with all kinds of advice for visitors including information on the Lambda Card which offers discounts at restaurants, bars and shops. COGAM also hosts a radio show, *Luna de Babilonia* (Monday 1000-1100, 108 FM); a TV show, *Hasta en las Mejores Familias* (Monday 1100, UHF 29); and runs several political social groups. The **Feministas Lesbianas de Madrid**, C Barquillo 44, **T** 91 319 36 89. Political feminist organization open to women only. **Gay Inform**, **T** 91 523 00 70.

## Bars and clubs

**Camp**, C Marqués de Valdeiglesias 6, **T** 91 531 92 15. *Metro Chueca. 1100-0330. Map 4, A10, p253* Superbly chic, glassy café-bar full of self-consciously beautiful people reclining on 70s-style furniture. Attracts a mixed crowd.

**Escape**, C Gravina 13. *Metro Chueca. Thu-Sat 2200-0500. Map 5, G4, p254* Lesbian bar with live shows on Friday and Saturday nights.

**Flamingo/Shangay Tea Dance**, C Mesonero Romanos 13, **T** 91 532 15 24. *Metro Callao* or *Gran Vía. Thu-Sun 2400-0600, plus after hours club. Map 4, A7, p253 Flamingo* has some of the best club nights in Madrid, including the gay/drag Shangay Tea Dance. Don't miss the Goa after hours club between 0600 and 1030 on Saturday and Sunday mornings.

**Mad Café**, C Virgen de los Peligros 4. *Metro Sevilla. Map 4, C9, p253* Multi-purpose café-restaurant-bar with a terrace at the back.

**Medea**, C Cabeza 33. *Metro Lavapiés. Thu-Sat 2300-0500. Map 4, G7, p253* The biggest and best-known women's disco.

**El Mojito**, C Olmo 6. *Metro Lavapiés. Wed-Sun 2200-0300. Map 4, G8, p253* Excellent music, lively mixed crowd and a popular spot with the fashion pack.

**Refugio**, C Doctor Cortezo 1, **T** 91 523 46 89. *Metro Tribunal. Mon-Sat 2400-0600, Sun 2100-0200. Map 6, e8, P256* Big, popular gay disco. Sweet on Thursday is a buzzy new club night, which attracts a mixed crowd.

**Rick's**, C Clavel 8. *Metro Gran Vía or Sevilla. 2300-0600. Map 4, A9, p253* Massively popular bar, especially at weekends.

**La Sastrería**, C Hortaleza 74, **T** 91 532 07 71. *Metro Tribunal. Mon-Thu 1000-0200, Fri 1000-0300, Sat 1100-0300, Sun 1100-0400. Map 5, G4, p254* A real classic on the gay scene, this charming former tailor's (hence the name) is great for drinks and snacks.

**Week End/Ohm/Bash**, Plaza Callao 4, www.tripfamily.com *Metro Callao. Thu-Sun 2400-0500. Map 4, A6, p254* Same place, different club nights. One of the best venues in Madrid, with pumping music, go-go dancers and a mixed, slickly dressed clientele.

---

## Bookshops

**A Different Life**, C Pelayo 30, www.lifegay.com *Metro Chueca. Map 5, G4, p254* Books, CDs and gifts, with a sister store close by for lingerie and cosmetics.

**Berkana**, C Gravina 11. *Metro Chueca. Map 5, G4, p254* A gay bookstore, which also has a good section of magazines.

## Cafés

**Acuarela**, C Gravina 10, **T** 91 522 21 43. *Metro Chueca.*
*1500-0300. Map 5, G5, p254* Nymphs, cherubs, candlelight and
candelabras, as well as great cocktails. Get there early to get a seat.

**Café Antik**, C Hortaleza 4, **T** 91 522 21 43. *Metro Gran*
*Vía. Tue-Sun 1700-0200. Map 4, A8, p253* Flamboyant new
café-bar painted in eye-popping colours and specialises in
Caribbean cocktails like caipirinhas and mojitos.

**Café Figueroa**, C Augusto Figueroa 17, **T** 91 521 16 73. *Metro*
*Chueca. Mon-Thu 1200-0100, Fri-Sat 1200-0230, Sun 1600-0100.*
*Map 5, G/H, p254* An elegant 19th-century café which has become
a classic on the gay scene; a great first-stop in Madrid.

**Mamá Inés Café**, C Hortaleza 22, **T** 91 522 72 95. *Metro Gran Vía.*
*Mon-Sat 1000-2400, Sun 1000-1500. Map 4, A9, p253* Good food.

## Hotels and hostales

Most hotels in the Chueca area (see p124) are gay-friendly, even if
they aren't gay owned. The following hotels are popular with gay
travellers. For price categories, see p115.

**B Hotel Atlántico**, Gran Vía 38, **T** 91 522 64 80, **F** 91 531 02 10.
*Metro Callao. Map 4, A6/7, p252/253* This is plush and gay-friendly
(although the clientele are predominantly straight). In a grand
19th-century mansion, close to Chueca.

**C Hotel Hispa Domus**, C San Bartolomé 4, 2°, **T** 91 523 81 27,
**F** 91 701 01 14, info@hispadomus.com, www.hispadomus.com/
*Metro Chueca. Map 4, A9, p253* Bright, modern decor, very helpful
staff at this gay *hostal* close to the nightlife of Chueca.

**D-E Hostal Hispano Hortaleza**, C Hortaleza 38 2-A, **T** 91 531 48 71, **F** 91 521 87 80. *Metro Chueca. Map 5, H3, p254* Two-star *hostal* in the heart of Chueca, with good value rooms decorated with dark wooden furniture and new bathrooms.

**D-E Hostal Puerta del Sol**, Puerta del Sol 14, 4°, **T** 91 522 51 26, **F** 91 522 98 15, www.hostalpuertadelsol.com *Metro Sol. Map 4, C7, p253* Very eager to please staff at this gay *hostal* overlooking the Puerta del Sol. Laundry and sitting room. Minimum two-night stay. Some en suite rooms.

**E Hostal Odesa**, C Hortaleza 38, 3°, **T/F** 91 521 03 38. *Metro Gran Vía. Map 5, H3, p254* Traditional decor and a mixed gay/straight clientele at this centrally located *hostal*. Some en suite rooms.

## Restaurants

**El Armario**, C San Bartolomé 7, **T** 91 532 83 77. *Metro Chueca. Mon-Sat 1330-1600 and 2100-2400, closed Aug. Map 5, H4, p254* Excellent cuisine, drag shows and kinky decor. Mainly gay clientele. There's a good value lunch menu, but prices are higher in the evenings.

**Divina La Cocina**, C Colmenares 13, **T** 91 531 37 65. *Metro Chueca. Mon 1330-1600, Tue-Thu 2100-2400, Fri-Sat 1330-1630 and 2100-2445. Map 4, A10, p253* A delightful restaurant serving excellent international cuisine in quirky, original surroundings.

**Gula Gula**, Gran Vía 1, **T** 91 522 87 64. *Metro Banco de España. Mon-Thu 1230-1600 and 2000-2400, Fri-Sat 1230-1600 and 2000-0200, Sun 2000-2400. Map 4, B10, p253* Fun, enormously popular drag show in the evening, plus lunchtime salad buffets. Booking essential. Also has a branch on Calle Infantes (see p135).

**Chez Pomme**, C Pelayo 4, **T** 91 532 16 46. *Metro Chueca.*
*Mon-Sat 1330-1600 and 2030-2330. Closed Aug.* *Map 5, H4, p254*
Charming, excellent value vegetarian restaurant in the heart
of Chueca.

**Sarrasín**, C Libertad 8, **T** 91 532 73 48. *Metro Chueca.* *Mon-Sat*
*1200-1600 and 2100-2400, closed first 2 weeks in Aug.* *Map 4, A10,*
*p253* Welcoming stylish café and restaurant, which is very popular
for its set price menu, available lunchtime and evening. Book in
advance.

The Spanish love children and you'll find yours are treated indulgently wherever you go and however badly they behave. Most museums offer free admission to children under four and reduced admission for those aged four and above. Public transport is free for children under four. You'll find everything you need (nappies, formula milk etc) in the local supermarkets and chemists, but bear in mind that almost everything is closed on Sundays. Restaurants and bars are child-friendly, which means that if your children can stay up late, you can take them wherever you go in the evening. Festivals usually offer fireworks, flame throwers and parades that kids love (although babies may not like the sheer amount of noise from firecrackers on New Year's Eve); check the festival listings on p181. Teenagers will love shopping at the Mercado de Fuencarral (see p190), which is a Mecca for young hipsters looking for their first tattoo.

## Childminding facilities

**Guardería Infantil El Carmen**, Gran Vía San Francisco 9, **T** 91 366 04 66.

**El Descanso de Mamá**, Condes de Torreanaz 4, **T** 91 574 39 94. Offers service of looking after and entertaining your children as long as you need them to – even all night, if necessary.

## Museums and sights

**Museo de Cera**, Paseo de Recoletos 41, **T** 91 308 08 25. *Metro Colón. Closed Mon. Map 5, F8, P255* The rather dull exhibits at the wax museum probably won't interest children as much as the chamber of horrors and simulator ride.

**Museo Thyssen-Bornemisza** (see p39) has family visits for children aged between six and 12 on Saturday and Sunday at 1000, 1200 and 1630. They are usually in Spanish, but you might be lucky and get an English-speaking tour guide.

**Museo Ejército** (see p 42) is a big favourites with Madrileño dads and their sons. See the models, uniforms, globes and lots of pistols, swords and daggers.

**Faro de Moncloa**, corner of Av de los Reyes Católicos and Plaza del Arco de la Victoria, **T** 91 544 81 04. *Metro Moncloa. Tue-Fri 1000-1400 and 1700-1900, Sat-Sun 1030-1730.* A 92-m tower with a glass lift that shoots up to an observation platform. Close to the child-friendly **Museo de América** (see p83).

**IMAX Madrid**, Parque Tierno del Galván, **T** 91 467 48 00. *1100-2215, special show at 2400 on Sat. Tickets available from Servicaixa,* **T** *902 33 22 11 (24 hr) or from box office. Tickets from*

Kids

€6.60; Mon €5.40. Dolphins, dinosaurs and adventures in space on an enormous screen.

**Museo Nacional Centro de Arte Reina Sofía** The contemporary art (see p37) usually appeals to arty teenagers, especially the art installations in the stunning Palacio de Cristal (see p44).

**Planetario de Madrid**, Parque Tierno Galván, **T** 91 467 38 98. Metro Méndez Álvaro. *Tue-Fri 1730-1845, Sat, Sun and public holidays 1130, 1245, 1730, 1845, 2000. €3/1.22 for under-14s.* Planetarium with shows in Spanish.

**Museo de Real Madrid**, Estadio Santiago Bernabeu, Puerta 3. *Metro Santiago Bernabeu. Closed Mon.* A must for football-crazy children; see under Parque de Atracciones below.

**Zoo-Aquarium de la Casa de Campo**, **T** 91 512 37 80. *Metro Batán. 1000-sunset. €12.15, children €9.80.* Small, well-kept zoo and aquarium, good for younger children.

## Parks

**Casa de Campo** (see p82). Huge rambling park, with walking and cycling paths, a boating lake, plus the Parque de Atracciones and zoo-aquarium (see above for both).

## Theme parks and funfairs

**Aquópolis**, Villanueva de la Cañada, Carretera de la Coruña (N-IV) Km 25, **T** 91 815 69 11, www.aquopolis.es/villanueva *Free bus from the Plaza España, Mon-Fri 1100 and 1200, Sat-Sun 1100, 1200, 1300.* Europe's biggest water park with dozens of log flumes, including the Black Hole and the almost-vertical Super Slide, as well as a wave pool and a smaller lake full of activities for younger children.

**El Parque de Atracciones de Madrid**, Casa de Campo, **T** 91 536 80 31, www.parquedeatracciones.es *Metro Batán*. All-inclusive ticket prices: €19.50 for over-7s, €11.50 for under-7s. Entrance plus two attractions €9. Entrance only, €4.50. Tickets for each attraction cost €1.50; over-7s need 2 tickets per attraction. Rides, rollercoasters, a special section for very little kids and a new exhibit-museum on Real Madrid to celebrate their 100th anniversary in 2002. Right next to the zoo-aquarium.

**Warner World**, San Martín de la Vega (22 km southeast of Madrid on the N-IV), www.warnerbrospark.com *Trains leave from Atocha*. Huge new theme park which opened in mid-2002: eight massive white-knuckle rides, water rides, a dedicated zone for toddlers and flight simulators. Signs and shows are all in Spanish.

## Trips

**The Strawberry Train** is a real steam engine that puffs along to Aranjuez (see p110) and has costumed attendants handing out huge strawberries on the journey.

**Teleférico**, Paseo Pintor Rosales s/n, **T** 91 541 74 50. *Metro Argüelles. Map 2, C1, p248* This cable car sways across from the Paseo Pintor Rosales out to the middle of the Casa de Campo park.

**Kids**

# Directory

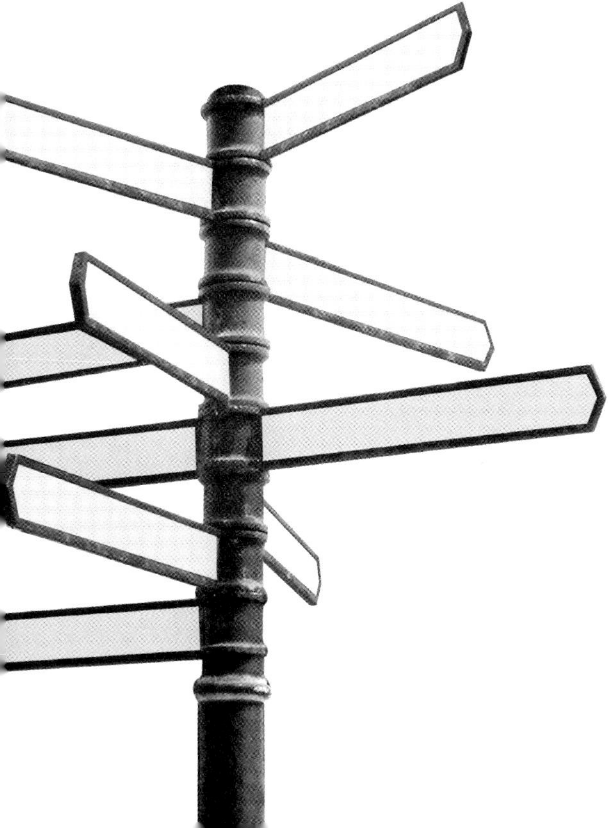

## Airline offices

**Air Europa**, Barajas Airport, T 902 401 501. **Air France**, C Princesa 1, T 91 541 96 81. **Air Lingus**, Gran Vía 88, T 91 541 42 16. **American Airlines**, C Pedro Texeira 8, T 91 597 07 39. **British Airways**, C Serrano 60, T 91 577 84 89. **Iberia**, C Velázquez 130, T 91 411 11 55.

## Banks and ATMs

Banks and ATMS are everywhere. You'll find several banks on the Puerta del Sol, the Gran Vía and around the Plaza España. They are usually open Mon- Fri 0830-1400. Some of the main branches open on Sat mornings from 0830-1300 (though not generally in Aug).

## Bicycle hire

**Ciclobike**, C Rumanía 5, T 91 775 58 24. Metro Antón Martín. Bike sales, rental and repairs. **Bicimanía**, C Palencia 20, T 91 533 11 89, www.bicimania.com Metro Alvarado. Rents and repairs bicycles.

## Car hire

Offices of the major car rental companies can be found at the airport and the two main train stations, Atocha and Chamartín. **Avis**, T 902 135 531, www.avis.com **Budget**, T 91 393 72 16, www.budget.es **Economy**, T 0845 4500877 (must be pre-booked before arrival), www.economycarhire.com **Europcar**, T 91 393 72 35, www.europcar.com **Hertz**, T 91 393 82 65, www.hertz.com **National** T 902 100 101, www.national.com, www.atesa.es

## Credit card lines

If your cards are lost or stolen: **American Express**: T 900 994 426. **Diner's Club**: T 902 40 11 12. **MasterCard/Visa**: T 900 971 231.

## Cultural institutions

**British Council**, Information and Study Centre, Paseo del General Martínez Campos 31, T 91 337 35 00, www.britishcouncil.es

**Goethe Institute**, C Zurbarán 21, T 91 391 39 44, www.goethe.de/wm/mad **Alliance Française**, C Velázquez 94, T 91 435 15 32, www.alliancefrancaisemadrid.net Metro Núñez de Balboa.

## Dentists

Dentistry is not covered by the UK's E111 agreement and treatment can be expensive. The following are English-speaking: **Clínica Dental Cisne**, C Magallanes 18. Metro Quevedo, T 91 446 3221; and **Dr Eduardo Fernández Blanco**, Av de América 4, bajo D, T 91 725 21 72.

## Disabled

Relatively few museums, hotels and restaurants are fully wheelchair accessible and it is usually best to call in advance to confirm what facilities are on offer. The three big museums – the Prado, the Reina Sofía and the Thyssen, are all wheelchair-accessible. The Metro map (available free at all stations, or online at www.Metromadrid.es) marks stations with wheelchair access. Almost half of the city's buses are now accessible to disabled travellers; they can be identified by the sign 'piso bajo'. For more information contact: **ALPE Turismo para Todos**, C Casarrubuelos 5, T 91 448 08 64, which publishes a useful hotel guide listing facilities for disabled travellers. **Federación de Minusválidos Físicos de la Comunidad de Madrid**, C de Galileo 69, T 91 593 35 50, information service T 91 447 54 99, www.servico.es/famma

## Doctors

EU residents are entitled to health care in the state hospitals but this is still a complicated process and you will need to get the E111 form before you leave your home country. The following are English-speaking doctors: **Dr Enrique Puerta Scott**, C San Francisco de Sales 36, T 91 534 58 11/649 280 952; and **Dr Niko Mihic,** C Lagasca 104, T 617 041 936, mihic@spainmeds.com

## Electricity

The current in Spain is 220V 50hz. North American appliances will require a special transformer and UK plugs will need a two-pin adaptor, available from Madrid's department stores.

## Embassies

**Australia**, Paseo de la Castellana 143, T 91 579 04 28, F 91 570 02 04, www.embaustralia.es  Metro Cuzco. **Canada**, C Núñez de Balboa 35, T 91 431 43 00, F 91 431 23 67, www.canada-es.org Metro Núñez de Balboa. **Ireland**, C Claudio Coello 73, T 91 576 35 00, F 91 435 16 77. Metro Serrano. **New Zealand**, Plaza de la Lealtad 2, T 91 523 02 26, F 91 523 01 71. Metro Banco de España. **UK**, C Fernando el Santo 19, T 91 319 02 00, F 91 319 04 23. Metro Alonso Martínez. **US**, C Serrano 75, T 91 577 40 00, F 91 577 57 35, www.embusa.es/  Metro Rubén Darío.

## Emergency numbers

There is a single number in Madrid for all emergency services (ambulance, fire and police): T 112.

## Hospitals

**Hospital Clínico Universitario San Carlos**, C Profesor Martín Lagos s/n, T 91 330 30 00 /91 330 30 01 (open 24 hrs), www. msc.es/insalud/hospitales/hcsc  **Hospital General Gregorio Marañón**, C Dr Esquerdo 46, T 91 586 80 00, www.hggm.es Metro O'Donnell. **Hospital La Princesa del Insalud**, C Diego de León 62, T 91 520 22 00, www.hup.es  Metro Diego de León.

## Internet/email

**Bigg**, C Alcalá 21, www.bbgigg.com  Huge internet café with prices which fluctuate according to demand; €1 will get you about 30-40 mins. **EasyEverything**, C Montera 10, T 91 523 29 44. Metro Sol. Prices fluctuate according to demand: €1.50-3 an hour. Open 24 hrs. **Work Center**, C Alberto Aguilera 1, T 91 448 78 77. Metro

Argüelles. Internet access €6 an hour. Macs and PCs. Other facilities. Open 24 hours.

## Language schools
**Acento Español**, C Mayor 4, 6º9, T 91 521 36 76, acentoes@ teleline.es Intensive and general courses, preparation for official DELE exam. Accommodation arranged. **Amerispan**, T 215 751 1100, T 1800 8796640 (USA), www.amerispan.com, has a school for 500 students in the centre of Madrid. **CEE Idiomas**, C Carmen 6, T 91 522 04 72, cee1@arrakis.es Courses for all levels, preparation for DELE and cultural activities. **Enforex**, Alberto Aguilera 26, T 91 594 37 76, www.enforex.com, has small classes that run throughout the year.

## Launderette
**Ondablu**, C León, www.ondablu.com Metro Antón Martín. New launderette offering service washes or do-it-yourself.

## Left luggage
Lockers at Atocha and Chamartín stations. Open 0600-2200.

## Lost property
For general lost property, T 91 588 43 46. For objects lost on the Metro or taxis, call T 91 588 43 44 or visit the 'Objetos Perdidos' office on Plaza Legazpi 7. For lost property on buses, T 91 406 88 10 or visit the office at C Alcántara 24, T 91 406 88 10.

## Media
The best and bestselling newspaper in Spain is the left-leaning *El País*, closely followed by the conservative daily *El Mundo*. *El Mundo* produces a useful listings section for Madrid with the Fri edition, as does *ABC*, another conservative daily. There are dozens of tabloid-style newspapers, many devoted exclusively to football. Spanish TV is largely an unending whirl of game shows, football,

psychic readings and late-night porn, but you might find a decent film on *TVE2* or *Canal Plus* although it will almost certainly be dubbed. The state-run radio stations include *RNE1* (88.2 FM) for news and current affairs programmes; *Radio Clásica* (96.5 FM) for classical music and Radio 3 (93.2 FM) for chart music.

The weekly listings magazine *Guía del Ocio* is available from kiosks and costs €1. It's exclusively in Spanish, but it's fairly easy to understand even for non-Spanish speakers and has TV schedules and radio frequencies at the back. It's better for cultural listings and don't expect it to have any of the latest clubs. To find out what's happening in Madrid's nightlife scene, head for almost any bar in Chueca and pick up some leaflets and freebie magazines. The free English language newspaper *InMadrid* has good bar and club listings, and *El Duende*, a free magazine (in Spanish only), is pretty useful thanks to the maps at the back.

### Opticians
**MultiOpticas**, Gran Vía 15, T 91 521 12 12. There are several branches of this large opticians all over the city.

### Pharmacies (late night)
All pharmacies have a list of the closest 24-hour chemists in their windows. The following are open 24 hours a day, 365 days a year: **Real Botica de la Reina Madre**, C Mayor 59, T 91 548 00 14. Metro Opera. **Farmacia del Globo**, C Atocha, 46, T 369 20 00. Metro Antón Martín, T 91 369 20 00. **Farmacia Goya 89**, C Goya 89, T 91 435 49 58. Metro Goya. **Farmacia de la Paloma**, C Toledo 46, T 91 365 34 58. Metro La Latina.

### Police
In emergencies call T 112. Each district has its own police station or Comisaría. You will have to report crimes or accidents for insurance purposes, but it's a painfully slow process and few police speak English. The most central police stations are: **Comisaría Centro**,

C Leganitos 19, T 91 548 79 85. **Comisaría Fuencarral**, C Gonzo de Limio 35, T 91 378 24 60. **Comisaría Retiro**, C Huertas 76, T 91 322 34 00.

## Post offices
Post boxes, marked *Correos y Telégrafos*, are yellow. Most tobacconists (*estancos*, marked with a brown-and-yellow symbol) sell stamps. You can send or receive faxes from any post office. The main post office is the **Palacio de Comunicaciones**, Plaza de Cibeles, T 91 521 65 00, information T 902 19 71 97, www.correos.es
Open Mon-Fri 0830-2130, Sat 0930-2130, Sun 0830-1400.

## Public holidays
On public holidays many bars and restaurants close down, as do most shops. The transport system runs restricted services. Some of these public holidays are celebrated with some of the city's best festivals. **Año Nuevo**, New Year's Day (1 Jan), **Epifanía** (6 Jan), Mar/Apr **Viernes Santo** (Good Friday), **Día del Trabajo**, Labour Day (1 May ), **Fiesta de la Comunidad de Madrid** (2 May), **Asunción** (15 Aug), **Día de la Hispanidad**, Colombus Day (12 Oct), **Día de Todos los Santos**, All Saints' Day (1 Nov), **Día de la Constitución**, Constitution Day (6 Dec), **Inmaculada Concepción**, Immaculate Conception (8 Dec), **Navidad**, Christmas Day (25 Dec).

## Religious services
**British Embassy Church of St George**, C Núñez de Balboa 43, T 91 576 51 09. Sun Church of England services 0830 and 1100. **Imanuel Baptist Church**, C Hernández de Tejada 4, T 91 407 43 47. Sun service 1100 and 1900. **Synogogue**, C Balmes 3, T 91 591 31 31. Fri service 1930.

## Telephone
Most public payphones, which you'll find on almost every street

corner, will accept coins and pre-paid telephone cards: most newsagents, post offices and tobacconists sell pre-paid phonecards in denominations of €5, 10, 15 and 20. Calls are cheaper after 2000 during the week and all day at weekends. Telephones in bars and cafés usually have more expensive rates than public payphones. Telephone centres (*locutorios*) are the cheapest method for calling abroad; you'll find them in the Atocha and Chamartín train stations and several smaller ones dotted throughout Chueca and Lavapiés.

## Time
Local time is one hour ahead of GMT/UTC, six hours ahead of US Eastern Standard Time and nine hours ahead of Pacific Standard Time. Clocks go forward one hour on the last Sun in Mar and back one hour on the last Sun in Oct (as in the UK).

## Toilets
Public toilets are few and far between, but most bars and cafés don't mind if you use theirs. The big department stores like *El Corte Inglés* have toilets.

## Transport enquiries
Call the transport information line, T 91 580 19 80, or see www.ctm-madrid.es   For genereral train information, call T 902 24 02 02.

## Travel agents
The *El Corte Inglés* department store has travel agents; they are expensive, but are efficient and very reliable. **Eurojoven**, Gran Vía 69, 1°, T 91 522 11 70. Specialists in youth travel. Student and youth travel.

# A sprint through history

| | |
|---|---|
| **Circa 400** | The Visigoths cross the Pyrenees and sweep down through the peninsula. They occupy most of the settlements in the region around present-day Madrid, including Toledo and Segovia. |
| **412** | The Visigoths establish Toledo as their capital. |
| **711** | A Muslim Berber army from North Africa crosses the Straits of Gibraltar. |
| **Circa 700-800** | The Visigothic empire crumbles as the Moors (as the Berbers are known) march steadily northwards. Christian armies gather in northern Spain and the Reconquista, (Reconquest), is launched. |
| **Circa 860** | Emir Mohammed I constructs a fortress on a cliffedge overlooking the Manzanares River. The new settlement which grows up around it is called Majrit, the origin of the name Madrid. |
| **1083** | Alfonso VI of Castile recaptures Majrit/Madrid once and for all. |
| **1085** | The Christian armies recapture Toledo, the first great victory of the Reconquista. |
| **1202** | Madrid is granted its *fueros* (a municipal charter). |
| **1309** | The Cortes (royal court and parliament) meets in Madrid for the first time. During this period, the Castilian court and parliament had no permanent home and met in different towns across the region. |
| **1469** | Marriage of Isabella I of Castile and Ferdinand V (Ferdinand II of Aragón); the joining of their kingdoms by marriage is traditionally considered to mark the birth of modern-day Spain. |

| | |
|---|---|
| **1478** | The Inquisition is established. |
| **1492** | The last Moorish kingdom, Granada, falls to the Castilian armies. The Jews are expelled from Spain. Columbus 'discovers' the Americas. |
| **1520** | The Revolt of the Comuneros: an uprising against the heavy taxes imposed by Carlos I (made Holy Roman Emperor as Charles V) is severely put down and the ringleaders are beheaded in Segovia. |
| **1561** | Felipe II establishes Madrid as the capital of the Spanish empire. |
| **1563-84** | The monastery of El Escorial is constructed outside Madrid. |
| **1588** | Defeat of the 'Invincible Armada'. |
| **1590-1619** | The Plaza Mayor is built. |
| **1656** | Pedro Texeira draws up his famous map of Madrid (a copy is in the Museo Municipal, see p79) |
| **1701-14** | War of the Spanish Succession; Charles of Habsburg is eventually defeated by the Bourbon claimant Philip of Anjou. |
| **1734** | The former Arabic fortress, since remodelled to become the Palacio Real, is destroyed by fire. |
| **1759-88** | Carlos III (nicknamed 'Madrid's first Mayor') embarks on a dramatic programme of public works; several important buildings, including the Prado, are erected in the late baroque style. |
| **1808** | Napoleonic armies march into Spain and Joseph Bonaparte is installed on the Spanish throne. The |

Madrileño uprising on 2 May is commemorated in Goya's paintings at the Prado.

**1833-1839** First Carlist War. This is another succession dispute, which breaks out when Ferdinand VII alters the law of succession in favour of his daughter, Isabel II. A faction supporting his brother Don Carlos rebel; they are put down but the Carlists remain a problem for Isabel throughout her reign.

**1835** The state confiscates church property in an attempt to fill its empty coffers.

**1898** Spanish-American War results in the loss of most of Spain's New World colonies. This shakes Spain's confidence and leads to a period of introspection which in turn leads to a cultural revival; in Madrid this era is sometimes called the Silver Age. Café society is at its height, with writers and politicians taking part in debates (*tertulias*) at Madrid's famous literary cafés.

**1936** A lengthy period of political turmoil is followed by the election of the Popular Front, made up of republicans, Socialists and Communists, in 1936. A military uprising precipitates the Spanish Civil War.

**March 1939** Madrid surrenders to the Nationalists.

**1939** The Nationalists under General Franco win the Civil War. Franco sets up a dictatorship.

**1975** Death of Franco and restoration of monarchy; Juan Carlos I is proclaimed king and immediately embarks on a programme of political reform.

| 1977 | The first democratic elections since 1936 are held, and Adolfo Suárez heads the new government. |
| 1978 | Spain becomes a constitutional monarchy. |
| 1981 | There is an attempted coup by right-wing army officials; Colonel Tejero and a group of civil guards burst into the Spanish Parliament firing pistols (Las Cortes, see p55). The uprising is rapidly put down. |
| 1982 | The socialist party of Felipe González is elected to government, with González as president. |
| 1986 | Spain joins the EC (now the EU). |
| 1991 | The conservative Partido Popular (PP) takes over Madrid's regional council. It begins a programme of belt-tightening that hits the arts particularly hard. |
| 1992 | Madrid is European Capital of Culture, Spain celebrates the 500th anniversary of Colombus' 'discovery' of the Americas, Expo is in Sevilla and Barcelona hosts the Olympics. |
| 1996 | The PP wins the general elections after scandal overwhelms the previous Socialist government and José María Aznar, a former tax-collector, becomes president. |
| 1 Jan 1999 | Spain joins the Euro. |
| 2000 | José María Aznar's PP wins the general elections for a second time. |
| 2002 | Spain holds the EU presidency and the euro replaces the peseta as Spain's national currency. |

# Art and architecture

**Until 5th century AD**
The most spectacular legacy of the Roman occupation is the vast aqueduct in Segovi.

**6th-8th century Visigothic**
The Visigoths left no trace in Madrid, but Toledo became the Visigothic capital in 412 and a small museum of Visigothic art is held in the church of San Román. Many of Toledo's churches contain recycled Visigothic elements. Bold lines, flat planes and strong colours characterize the painting, while the few sculptural pieces that survive are stylized and almost abstract.

**8th-15th century Moorish**
Art and architecture achieved spectacular new heights under the Moors. Architects trained in Damascus introduced the use of horseshoe arches and a rich decorative style using brilliantly coloured tiles (*azulejos*) in abstract patterns, and the intricate coffered (*artesanado*) ceilings. The best examples of Moorish art and architecture in the Madrid region are in Toledo, but almost nothing remains of the Moorish settlement of Mayrit apart from a stretch of wall next to the cathedral, and the tower attached to the church of San Nicolás de las Servitas. The work of Christian artists under Moorish rule is known as mozarabic, and the work of Muslims who remained in the area after the Reconquest is known as mudéjar.

**11th-13th century Romanesque**
Romanesque art flourished in northern Spain and there are very few examples in the Madrid region apart from a handful of typically austere Romanesque churches in Avila and Segovia.

| | |
|---|---|
| **13th-15th century Gothic** | As the influence of the Moors waned, Romanesque gave way to Gothic, which was largely imported from France. The Castilian Gothic style developed in two directions: the deliberately austere, plain style which characterises Segovia's cathedral (p100); and a highly decorative style which developed into Isabelline Gothic, which you can see at Toledo's Monasterio de San Juan de los Reyes. Travelling artists introduced techniques of the Sienese School, and later on, Flemish naturalism and portrayals of the human figure began to display a meticulous attention to detail and realism. |
| **16th-17th century Renaissance and Golden Age** | In architecture, Isabelline Gothic led to the highly ornamental Plateresque (from *plateros* meaning silversmith) style, in which sculptural detailing, particularly around the doorways, contrasted with the simple lines of the rest of the building. The great architect of the Renaissance was Juan de Herrera (1530-97), who built El Escorial for Felipe II (see p97) and whose austere, classical style would influence most of the Habsburg architecture in Madrid. By the 17th century Madrid had taken over from Seville as the most important art centre in Spain and was ushering in its *Siglo de Oro* or Golden Age. This was the age of great Spanish painters like Zurbarán (1598-1664), Ribera (1591-1652), Murillo (1618-82), El Greco (1541-1614), who was Cretan by birth but moved to Toledo and, most importantly, Diego Rodríguez de Silva Velázquez (1599-1660). |

| | |
|---|---|
| **18th century baroque** | The florid embellishments and curved lines of the baroque style can be seen in the Catedral de San Isidro, the pretty 18th-century Basílica de San Miguel on Calle Mayor and Pedro de Ribera's exuberant portal on the Museo Municipal (see p79). Madrid's grandest example of baroque is the extravagant Palacio Real, with Tiepolo and Mengs frescoes. |
| **19th century** | In the late 19th century Madrid's richest citizens moved modern Salamanca. The greatest Spanish artist of this era was Francisco Goya (1746-1828), whose works are well represented at the Prado, the Academia de Bellas Artes and in the lovely Museo Panteón de Goya. |
| **20th century** | In architecture, this century was the age of the grand gesture: the broad, flashy Gran Vía; the enormous Edificio España, a monument to Francoism; and the skyscrapers built along the Paseo de la Castellana in the 1980s. Picasso and Dalí studied in Madrid but the arts stifled in Spain under Franco. From the 1960s Antonio López García and the group known as Realismo Madrileño, or Madrid Realism, began to gain some international acclaim. |
| **Post-Franco** | New buildings are flourishing; the latest is Rafael Moneo's subterranean extension to the Prado. Visit the Museo Nacional Centro de Reina Sofía, with exhibitions of the latest Spanish talent, or take a wander though the highly regarded annual contemporary art show, ARCO. |

# Books

**Fiction**

**de Cervantes**, M, *Don Quixote*. ( 2001), Penguin. One of the best-known Spanish novels; a rollicking read.

**Quevedo**, F, *The Swindler* (translated in *Two Spanish Picaresque Novels* (1969) Penguin. A classic picaresque tale of the rise and fall of the eponymous swindler; brilliantly told with chilling malice.

**Marías**, J, *Tomorrow in the Battle Think on Me and a Heart so White* (1996), Harvill Press. One of Spain's most brilliant contemporary novelists, beautifully translated by Margaret Jull Costa.

**Pérez-Reverte**, A, *The Flanders Panel* (1994), Harvill Press. A well-written highly entertaining suspense novel set in Madrid.

**Non-fiction**

**Hooper**, J, *The New Spaniards* (1995), Penguin. An updated version of his excellent portrait of Spain post-Franco, *Spaniards; A Portrait of the New Spain*.

**Jacobs**, M, *Madrid Observed*. (1996), Pallas Athene. An engaging, illuminating and entertaining book on walks around the city.

**Lalaguna**, J, *A Traveller's History of Spain* (2002), Windrush and Co. A bit dry and scholarly, but otherwise a good pocket-sized overview of the country's history.

**Nash**, E. *Cities of the Imagination: Madrid* (2001), Signal Books. An enjoyable cultural and literary companion, written with a deep, but clear-eyed, affection for the city.

# Language

## Pronunciation

The stress in a Spanish word conforms to one of three rules: 1) if the word ends in a vowel, or in n or s, the accent falls on the penultimate syllable (*ventana*, *ventanas*); 2) if the word ends in a consonant other than n or s, the accent falls on the last syllable (*hablar*); 3) if the word is to be stressed on a syllable contrary to either of the above rules, the acute accent on the relevant vowel indicates where the stress is to be placed (*pantalón*). Unless listed below consonants can be pronounced in Spanish as they are in English.

b, v  Their sound is interchangeable and is a cross between the English 'b' and 'v'

c  Like English 'k', except before 'e' or 'i' when it is as the 'th' in English 'thimble'

g  Hard like English 'game' or 'got' before 'a' or 'o', soft before 'e' and 'i' like the 'ch' in 'loch'

h  Never pronounced except in combination 'ch' when it sounds like English chimney

j  As the 'ch' in the Scottish 'loch'

ll  As the 'y' in 'Yolanda' or the 'lli' in 'million'

ñ  as the 'ni' in English 'onion'

rr  Trilled much more strongly than in English

z  As the 'th' in English 'thistle/thimble'

---

## Greetings, courtesies

Hello/goodbye  *hola* (*diga* on telephone)/*adios*

please/thank you (very much)  *por favor*/*(muchas) gracias*

How are you?  *¿Cómo está?*/*¿Cómo estás?*

Please to meet you  *Mucho gusto/encantado/encantada*

What is your name?  *¿Cómo se llama?*

Do you speak English?  *¿Habla inglés?*

I don't speak Spanish  *No hablo español*

I don't understand  *No entiendo*
Please speak slowly  *Hable despacio por favor*

---

**Getting around**
airport  *el aeropuerto*
arrivals/departures  *las llegadas/salidas*
station  *la estación*
corner  *la esquina*
How do I get to_?  *¿Cómo llego a_?*
near/far  *cerca/lejos*
on the left/right  *a la izquierda/derecha*
straight on  *todo recto*
one-way/return  *de ida/de vuelta*
When does the next plane/train leave/arrive?  *¿Cuándo sale/llega el próximo avión/el tren?*
I want a ticket to_  *Quiero un billete a_*
Where is_?  *¿Dónde está_?*

---

**Accommodation**
Do you have a room for two people?  *¿Tiene una habitación para dos personas?*
Can I see the room?  *¿Podría ver la habitación?*
with shower/bath  *con ducha/baño*
with two beds/a double bed  *con dos camas/una cama matrimonial*
air conditioning/heating  *aire acondicionado/calefacción*
toilet paper  *el papel higiénico*

---

**Shopping**
open/closed  *abierto/cerrado*
How much does it cost?  *¿Cuánto cuesta?*
change  *cambio*
cheap/expensive  *barato/caro*
credit card  *la tarjeta de crédito*
travellers' cheques  *los cheques de viajero*

post office *correos*
postcards/stamps *postales/sellos*

---

## Eating out
breakfast *desayuno*
lunch *almuerzo*
dinner *cena*
a table for two *una mesa para dos personas*
Can I see the menu? *¿Podría ver la carta por favor?*
fixed price menu *menú del día*
bill/check *la cuenta*
toilet/toilets *servicios/aseos*
men *señores/hombres/caballeros*
women *señoras/damas*
Is service included? *¿Está incluido el servicio?*
bread/butter/sandwich *pan/mantequilla/bocadillo*
water (mineral sparkling/still) *agua (mineral con gas/sin gas)*
beer *cerveza*
wine (red, white) *vino (tinto, blanco)*
juice *zumo*

---

## Tapas
*aceitunas (rellenas)* (stuffed) olives
*albóndigas* meatballs
*almejas* clams
*anchoas* salted anchovies
*boquerones* pickled fresh anchovies
*chipirones* squid
*chorizo* spicy Spanish pork sausage
*croquetas de jamón/pollo/bacalao* croquettes with ham/chicken/cod
*empanadas* pies
*gambas a la plancha* grilled shrimp, prawns
*gambas al ajillo* prawns in garlic

*huevos revueltos*  scrambled eggs
*patatas bravas*  chunks of fried potato, served with a spicy sauce
*pimientos asados/rebozados*  roast red peppers/fried in light batter
*surtido de queso/jamón*  platter of cheeses or ham
*tortilla*  thick fried potato omelette

### *Pescado*  Fish
*atún*  tuna
*bacalao*  cod
*calamares*  squid
*gambas*  prawns
*lubina*  sea bass
*mariscos*  shellfish
*mejillones*  mussels
*pez espada*  swordfish
*pulpo*  octopus

### *Carne*  Meat
*carne de vaca*  beef
*cabrito*  kid
*cerdo*  pork
*chorizo*  spiced sausage
*cocido*  Madrileño stew of meat, chickpeas and vegetables
*cochinillo*  roast suckling pig
*conejo*  rabbit
*cordero*  lamb
*jamón serrano*  cured mountain ham
*morcilla*  blood sausage
*pollo*  chicken
*salchichón*  salami
*solomillo*  pork sirloin

### *Verduras and legumbres*  Vegetables and legumes
*alcachofas*  artichokes

*arroz*  rice
*cebolla*  onion
*champiñones*  button mushrooms
*espárragos*  asparagus
*espinacas*  spinach
*garbanzos*  chickpeas
*judías (verdes)*  beans (French)
*lechuga*  lettuce
*patatas (fritas)*  potatoes (fried)
*setas*  wild mushrooms

### *Fruta* Fruit
*fresa*  strawberry
*manzana*  apple
*melocotón*  peach
*naranja*  orange
*piña*  pineapple
*plátano*  banana
*uva*  grape

# Index

# Credits

**Footprint credits**

Text editors: Jo Williams, Claire Boobbyer and Stephanie Lambe
Series editor: Rachel Fielding
Editorial assistant: Ed Gowan

Production: Jo Morgan, Mark Thomas
In-house cartography: Sarah Sorensen, Robert Lunn, Kevin Feeney, Claire Benison

Design: Mytton Williams
Maps: adapted from original cartography by Netmaps SA, Barcelona, Spain
Metro map: Metro de Madrid

**Photography credits**

Front cover: Alamy
Inside: Cathryn Kemp
Generic images: John Matchett
Back cover: Cathryn Kemp

**Print**

Manufactured in Italy by Rotolito Lombarda, Italy

**Publishing information**

Footprint Madrid
1st edition
Text and maps © Footprint Handbooks Ltd November 2002

ISBN 1 903471 47 8
CIP DATA: a catalogue record for this book is available from the British Library

® Footprint Handbooks and the Footprint mark are a registered trademark of Footprint Handbooks Ltd

Published by Footprint Handbooks
6 Riverside Court
Lower Bristol Road
Bath, BA2 3DZ, UK
T +44 (0)1225 469141
F +44 (0)1225 469461
E discover@footprintbooks.com
W www.footprintbooks.com

Distributed in the USA by
Publishers Group West

Publishing stuff

# Complete title list

## Latin America & Caribbean

Latin America & Caribbean
Argentina
Barbados (P)
Bolivia
Brazil
Caribbean Islands
Central America & Mexico
Chile
Colombia
Costa Rica
Cuba
Cusco & the Inca Trail
Dominican Republic
Ecuador & Galápagos
Handbook
Guatemala Handbook
Havana (P)
Mexico
Nicaragua
Peru
Rio de Janeiro
South American
Handbook
Venezuela

## North America

Vancouver (P)
Western Canada

## Africa

Cape Town (P)
East Africa
Libya
Marrakech &
the High Atlas
Morocco
Namibia
South Africa
Tunisia
Uganda

## Middle East

Egypt
Israel
Jordan
Syria & Lebanon

## Asia

Bali
Bangkok & the Beaches
Cambodia
Goa
India
Indian Himalaya
Indonesia
Laos
Malaysia
Myanmar (Burma)
Nepal
Pakistan
Rajasthan & Gujarat
Singapore
South India
Sri Lanka
Sumatra
Thailand
Tibet
Vietnam

## Australasia

Australia
New Zealand
Sydney (P)
West Coast Australia

## Europe

Andalucía
Barcelona
Berlin (P)
Bilbao (P)
Bologna (P)
Copenhagen (P)
Croatia
Dublin (P)
Edinburgh (P)
England
Glasgow
Ireland
London
Madrid (P)
Naples (P)
Northern Spain
Paris (P)
Reykjavik (P)
Scotland
Scotland Highlands &
Islands
Spain
Turkey

(P) denotes pocket
Handbook

# For a different view…
## choose a Footprint

Over 80 Footprint travel guides
Covering more than 145 of the world's most exciting
countries and cities in Latin America, the Caribbean, Africa, Indian
sub-continent, Australasia, North America, Southeast Asia, the
Middle East and Europe.

Discover so much more…
The finest writers.  In-depth knowledge.  Entertaining and accessible.
Critical restaurant and hotels reviews. Lively descriptions of all the
attractions. Get away from the crowds.

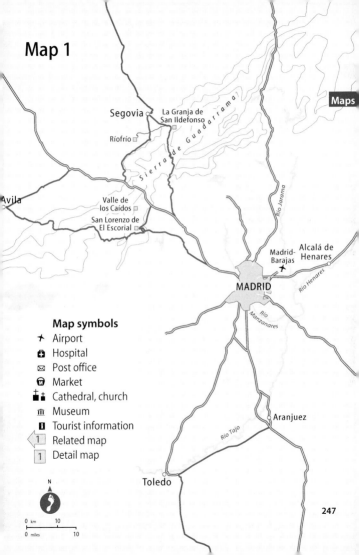

# Map 1

Segovia
La Granja de San Ildefonso
Ríofrío
Sierra de Guadarrama
Avila
Valle de los Caídos
San Lorenzo de El Escorial
Río Jarama
Madrid-Barajas
Alcalá de Henares
MADRID
Río Henares
Río Manzanares
Aranjuez
Río Tajo
Toledo

## Map symbols

✈ Airport
✚ Hospital
✉ Post office
🛒 Market
⛪ Cathedral, church
🏛 Museum
ℹ Tourist information
◁1 Related map
1 Detail map

N

0 km 10
0 miles 10

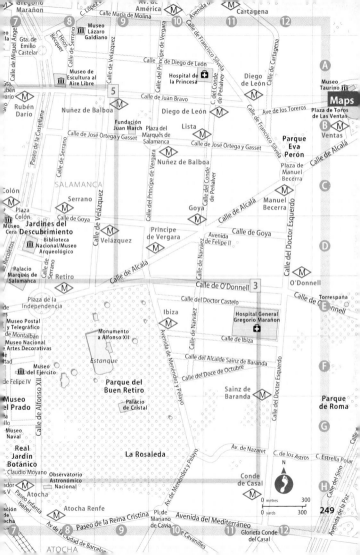

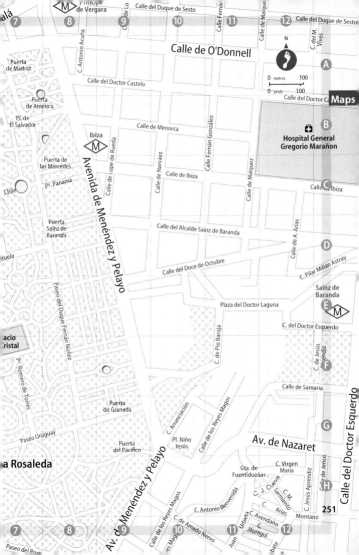

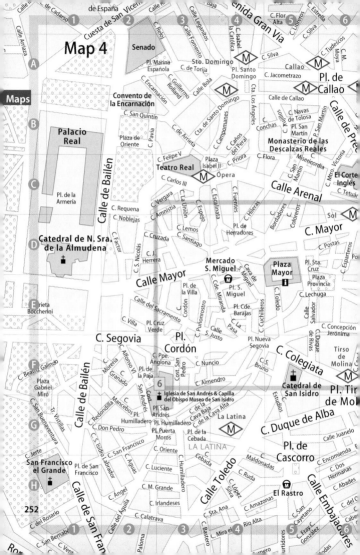

Map 4

de Cadarso
Cuesta de San Vicent...
de España
Calle Baja
Avenida Gran Vía
C. Flor Alta
C. Estrella

Calle Arrieta
① ② Calle Reloj ③ Calle Leganitos
Senado ④ C. Isabel la Católica
Sto. Domingo
C. Silva
Callao
⑥

Ⓐ Cuesta de San Vicent...
Pl. Marina Española
C. de Torija
Pl. Santo Domingo
Calle Fomento
C. Tudescos
Moya
C.M.
Pl. de Callao

Maps
Convento de la Encarnación
C. de Torija
Cta. de Santo Domingo
Calle de Callao
C. Jacometrazo
C. Silva

Ⓑ Palacio Real
C. San Quintín
C. de Pavía
Plaza de Oriente
C. de Arrieta
Campomanes
Caños del Peral
Conchas
C. Navas de Tolosa
Pl. San Martín
Monasterio de las Descalzas Reales
Calle de Pre...

C. Felipe V
Plaza Isabel II
Teatro Real
Ópera
Misericordia
C. San Martín
El Corte Inglés

Ⓒ Calle de Bailén
Pl. de la Armería
C. Carlos III
C. Vergara
C. La Unión
C. Escalinata
C. Fuentes
C. Hileras
C. Bordadores
C. Coloreros
Calle Arenal
C. Mtro. Victoria
C. Tetuár
Sol

Ⓓ Catedral de N. Sra. de la Almudena
C. Requena
C. Noblejas
C. Factor
C. Cruzada
C. Amnistía
C. Lemos
C. Santiago
Pl. de Herradores
C. Mayor
C. Postas
C. Esparteros

Ⓔ Rieta Boccherini
C.S. Nicolás
C. Herrera
C.J.
Calle Mayor
Pl. de la Villa
C. Cordón
Mercado S. Miguel
Cava de San Miguel
Pl. S. Miguel
C. Toledo
Plaza Mayor
Pl. Sta. Cruz
Plaza Provincia
C. Lechuga
C. Concepción Jerónima

Ⓕ Beato.V. Galindo
Calle del Sacramento
C. Villa
Pl. Cruz Verde
Pl. Cordón
C. Cde. de Barajas
Cuchilleros
Calle Salvador
Plaza Gabriel Miró
C. Alfonso VI
C. Granado
Pl. de la Paja
Pje. Anglona
Cost. San Pedro
C. Nuncio
Pl. Nueva Segovia
C. Colegiata
Tirso de Molina

Ⓖ C. San Buenaventura
C. Morería
Redondilla
Mancebos
Pl. Humilladero
C. Don Pedro
6
Iglesia de San Andrés & Capilla del Obispo Museo de San Isidro
Pl. San Andrés
Pl. de la Cava Alta
Cava Baja
La Latina
Catedral de San Isidro
Pl. Tir de Mol
C. Duque de Alba

Ⓗ C. Jerte
San Francisco el Grande
Pl. de San Francisco
C. San Isidro Labrador
C. Aguas
C. San Francisco
C. Oriente
Pl. Puerta Moros
Pl. de la Cebada
Cebada
Maldonadas
C. Ruda
Calle Toledo
Pl. de Cascorro
C. Encomienda
C. Dos Hermanas
C. Abades

252
C. del Rosario
Calle de San Fran...
C. del Águila
C. Ángel
C. M. Grande
C. Irlandeses
C. Calatrava
C. Sta. Ana
C. Mira
C. Amazonas
C. López Silva
El Rastro
C. San Cayetano
C. Franc C. González
C. del C

① ② Paloma ③ ④ Río Alta ⑤ ⑥

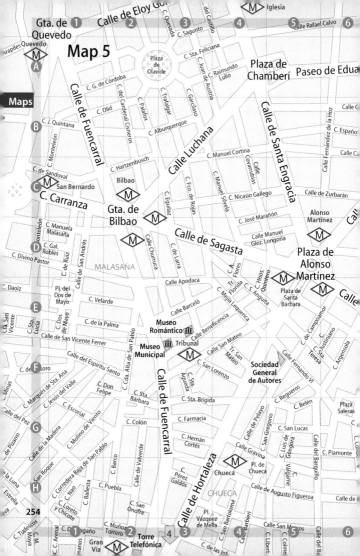

# Map 5

Gta. de Quevedo ❶

Calle de Eloy Go... ❷ ❸ ❹ C. Rafael Calvo ❺ ❻

Ⓜ Iglesia

Arapiles Quevedo

Ⓐ

C. Quesada

C. del Castillo

C. Sagunto

Plaza de Olavide

C. Sta. Feliciana

C. Juan de Austria

C. Raimundo Lulio

Plaza de Chamberí

Paseo de Edua...

Calle G...

Maps

C. G. de Córdoba

C. del Cardenal Cisneros

C. Olid

C. Palafox

C. Trafalgar

C. Garcilaso

Calle de Santa Engracia

Calle Fernández de la Hoz

C. Españo

Calle G

Ⓑ

C. J. Quintana

C. Alburquerque

Calle Luchana

C. Manuel Cortina

Calle de Zurbarán

Calle de Fuencarral

C. Monteleón

C. Hartzenbusch

Bilbao

C. F.co de Rojas

C. Manuel Silela

C. Nicasio Gallego

Calle Covarrubias

C. de Sandoval

Ⓒ Ⓜ San Bernardo

C. Carranza

Ⓜ Gta. de Bilbao

C. Eguilaz

C. José Marañón

Alonso Martínez

Ⓜ

C. Manuela Malasaña

Monteleón

C. de Ruiz

Ⓜ

Calle de Sagasta

Calle Manuel Glez. Longoria

Plaza de Alonso Martínez

Calle

Ⓓ C. Gal. Robles

C. Divino Pastor

Calle de San Andrés

C. Churruca

C. de Lara

C. A. Flores

C. Hnos. Quintero

Ⓜ

Plaza de Santa Bárbara

Ⓜ Calle

Daoiz

MALASAÑA

Pl. del Dos de Mayo

C. Velarde

Calle Apodaca

C. de la Florida

C. S. Anguita

C. de Campoamor

Ⓔ

C. Sta. Lucía

C. Dos de Mayo

Calle Barceló

Calle Mejía Lequerica

C. Justiniano

C. Sta. Teresa

C. Argensola

C. San Vicente

C. de la Palma

Calle de San Vicente Ferrer

Museo Romántico 🏛

Calle Beneficencia

Calle San Mateo

Sociedad General de Autores

Calle Fernando VI

Ⓕ C. de Toro

Calle del Espíritu Santo

Cda. Alta de San Pablo

C. Sta. Águeda

Museo Municipal 🏛

Ⓜ Tribunal

Tr. San Mateo

C. San Mateo

C. San Lorenzo

Minas

Calle del Pez

Ⓖ

C. Marqués de Sta. Ana

C. Jesús del Valle

C. Don Felipe

C. Molino de Viento

C. Sta. Brígida

C. San Lorenzo

Calle de Pizarro

C. de la Madera

C. Escorial

C. Colón

C. Farmacia

C. Requeros

C. Belén

Plaza Salesas

C. San Lucas

C. Luis de Góngora

C. del Barquillo

C. Piamonte

de la Luna

San Roque

Ⓗ

C. Corredera Baja de San Pablo

C. Barco

C. Valverde

C. Hernán Cortés

Calle de Pelayo

C. San Gregorio

C. de Góngora

la Luna

Estrella

C. Tudescos

254

C. M.

C. Moya

C. Arenal

C. Engaño

manos

❶

C. Nao

C. Loreto y Chicote

C. Ballesta

C. Puebla

C. San Onofre

C. Muñoz Torrero

❷ Torre Telefónica

Calle de Fuencarral

Calle de Hortaleza

Ⓜ Chueca

C. Pérez Galdós

Pl. de Chueca

CHUECA

Calle de Augusto Figueroa

Calle San Marcos

C. Valgame

C. Libert

C. Colme

❻

Pl. Vázquez de Mella

C. San Bartolomé

❸ ❹

C. de las In...

Calle del

Ⓜ Gran Vía

Calle Alfonso X

Calle

Calle de Fortuny

Gta. Rubén Darío

Rubén Darío

Calle Jénner

Museo de Escultura al Aire Libre

Calle de Maldonado

Calle de Juan Bravo

Núñez de Balboa

Calle de Padilla

C. M. de Villamejor

Fundación Juan March

C. Marqués de Riscal

Calle de José Ortega y Gasset

Paseo de la Castellana

Calle de Serrano

C. Mqués. de Villamagna

C. de Don Ramón de la Cruz

Calle de Monte Esquinza

Calle de Zurbarán

C. de Fortuny

Calle de Claudio Coello

Calle Lagasca

Calle de Núñez de Balboa

Blanca Navarra

Calle Fernando El Santo

C. de Ayala

Calle de Ayala

Orfila

C. Amador de los Ríos

SALAMANCA

C. Alcalá Galiano

Calle de Hermosilla

Calle de Hermosilla

nova

Colón

C. M. de Zurgena

Serrano

Calle de Velázquez

C. de Castelló

Orellana

Instituto Francés

Villa París

Museo Cera

Plaza Colón

Centro Cultural de la Villa

Calle de Goya

ganza

Jardines del Descubrimiento

Velázquez

y Baus

Almirante

Paseo de Recoletos

Biblioteca Nacional/ Museo Arqueológico

Calle de Jorge Juan

Calle de Jorge Juan

C. Mqués. de la Ensenada

Calle de Claudio Coello

C. Puigcerdà

Calle Gurtubay

Calle de Villanueva

N

C. Gil de Santiváñes

C. del Cid

Calle de Recoletos

0 metres 100

0 yards 100

Palacio Marqués de Salamanca

Calle Villalar

Calle de Columela

Calle de Alcalá

C. S. Olozaga

Plaza de la Independencia

Retiro

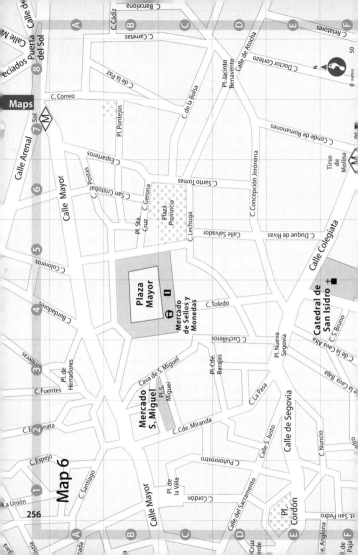